Philosophy and Educational Policy

A Critical Introduction

Christopher Winch and
John Gingell

 RoutledgeFalmer
Taylor & Francis Group

LONDON AND NEW YORK

First published 2004
by RoutledgeFalmer
2 Park Square, Milton Park, Abingdon, Oxfordshire, OX14 4RN

Simultaneously published in the USA and Canada
by RoutledgeFalmer
270 Madison Avenue, New York, NY 10016

RoutledgeFalmer is an imprint of the Taylor & Francis Group

© 2004 Christopher Winch and John Gingell

Typeset in Goudy by
Wearset Ltd, Boldon, Tyne & Wear
Printed and bound in Great Britain by
TJ International Ltd, Padstow, Cornwall

British Library Cataloguing in Publication Data
A catalogue record for this book is available
from the British Library

Library of Congress Cataloging in Publication Data
A catalog record for this book has been requested

ISBN 0-415-36957-6 (HBK)
ISBN 0-415-36958-4 (PBK)

Contents

Preface

Educational policy is based on ideas about human nature, about justice and about the purposes of education. These ideas are often not clearly articulated and can sometimes be hard to find behind the political rhetoric of pragmatism and the search for 'what works', as if policy-making were a neutral exercise like fixing a broken engine. But education is at least partly about the overall aims that society has for itself and how these aims are realised in practice. It cannot, therefore, be a neutral technical exercise, but is invariably a deeply political, ethical and cultural one, bound up with ideas about the good society and how lives can be worthwhile. We aim to uncover the philosophical thinking that underlies the formation of educational policy. When we first thought about this book, we realised that there are books on educational policy and books on educational ideas, but few, if any, that bring together policy and ideas in a way that is accessible to those studying philosophy for the first time, so our intention was to fill that gap in the literature.

Our motivation to do so was increased by the fact that there have been relatively few introductions to the philosophy of education in recent years and this at a time when educational policy is attracting attention world-wide. Education is seen, rightly or wrongly, as the key to the modernisation of traditional societies and as a way of equipping nations to compete in a globalised economy. The issues involved here are complex and subtle. This is not apparent at first glance, but once one begins to consider an educational policy issue in detail, all sorts of questions arise concerning the nature of particular societies, their aspirations, their ideas about justice and the way in which they attempt to deal with diversity. Our aim is to give the reader a sense of what the major issues are, and their ramifications for decisions about policy. If we manage to do that, then we will feel that we have succeeded.

Introduction

This is a book which seeks to introduce central questions in educational policy through engagement with their philosophical assumptions. It is, then, an introduction to central questions in the philosophy of education, as well as to central questions in educational policy. It also attempts to make these issues accessible to first- and second-year undergraduates. Over the years a number of introductions to the philosophy of education have been written in the English-speaking world. None of them have, however, to our knowledge had such an explicit engagement with the policy agenda.

One reason for this is that the analytical tradition of philosophy of education, to which the authors belong, has tended to think of education in a non-political way, as something that can be explained through the impartial examination of educational concepts that apply in all societies and at all times. However, this feature of the analytic tradition is radically misleading and has tended to obscure, rather than clarify, the central questions of education. Chief among these features is the assumption that education by its very nature is a good thing and that therefore there are no real substantive questions concerning the justification of educational policies which need to be asked or answered. So, for instance, this assumption avoids rather than deals with questions concerning the funding of education. It never asks whether, even if education is a good thing, the state should be committed to paying for it. It therefore ignores the fact that decisions concerning education are often political decisions and consequently the fact that our political views will influence both the questions that we ask and the answers that we will accept. It misses the obvious point that educational practices, of any sort, occur within specific cultural contexts and will be shaped by the cultural and moral values which constitute this context. It pays scant attention to the fact that consumers of education at every level, e.g. children, parents, employers, are working with sets of moral, political, economic and cultural values which must colour what they take to be educationally acceptable or unacceptable.

Partly, we think, such blindness to some of the real issues comes from confusing two different things; the first of these is the *concept* of education which, we shall argue, is relatively unproblematic and concerns what must occur in every society, namely, the preparation for adult life of future generations. The second is the different *conceptions* of education on offer which give substance to education in particular societies. Since these conceptions are often competing and conflicting, they always stand in need of justification and argument. Thus, we might ask whether education should be about preparation for work or for a life of leisure, and if it is about preparing for leisure for some, how shall we decide who shall be prepared for work and who for leisure? Or, to take another example, if one group within a society believes that a worthwhile life can be lived without religious belief, while another deems it absolutely essential for a worthwhile life that children are brought up with specific religious beliefs, how can these two apparently conflicting views be reconciled with each other, if, indeed, they can be reconciled at all?

To some extent, reluctance in the past on the part of philosophy of education to grapple with these issues has rested on an unwillingness to acknowledge that questions of educational value are always, in the end, enmeshed with our other values concerning religion, morality, social relationships, work, family life and individual freedom and that therefore no serious discussion of education can be held without some reference to these other values. In what follows we try to at least initiate the types of discussion that must underpin any realistic conception of education. In doing so we will pay particular attention to the kind of societies with which we are most familiar and where we expect most of our readership to be. These are the developed liberal democracies of Western Europe, North America and Australasia. In these societies we find democratic and parliamentary government, free economic markets and a relatively secular outlook. We hasten to add that what we have to say is not just relevant to these societies. Other societies outside these areas are interested in learning from them: how not to conduct themselves as well as the positive things that they think that they can learn from the practices of the liberal democracies. Therefore, this book should also be of use to anyone interested in the problems of education as they occur in liberal democracies. Thus, the conceptions of education that we are particularly concerned with arise within that sort of society and those conceptions in turn lead to particular educational problems that have policy implications for the political governance of education in those societies.

We begin by setting out the general problems that complex societies face in establishing a purpose for their educational systems given the facts of political and cultural diversity (Chapter 1). We then move on to deal with what we take to be the most important issues that arise from these general questions about purpose and value. So Chapter 2 deals with the issue of how aims and curricula are connected and how a satisfactory curriculum can be constructed. We then move on to deal with teaching and learning. In the background here are worries about whether learning requires teaching and, if so, what the relationship between the two is. Related to this is the evident tension between a desire to make young people independent individuals and make them self-teachers, with the desire to give young people a firm foundation of acquaintance with basic skills and the fundamental achievements of their cultures and the desire that they be independent, critical and innovative. Different societies take different views concerning whether they have achieved a balance between these two apparently conflicting imperatives.

We go on to consider in Chapter 4 what kind of teaching is most appropriate and whether or not we can produce evidence for what kind of teaching works and what does not. This concern is related to larger worries in some societies concerning whether their education systems are working properly and whether we would know if they were. The question of the 'right' kind of teaching method looms large in these discussions, but so do other matters. So, for instance, the increasing prominence of globalisation has brought in its train a series of concerns relating to the effectiveness of educational systems and issues to do with assessment and accountability. These issues receive detailed attention in Chapter 5. The individualistic nature of liberal democratic societies has brought into focus the need to reconcile individual aspirations with social solidarity. Moral, social and civic education are thought to be, in their different ways, means of addressing these conflicts and are the subject of Chapter 6. In addition, the aspiration in these societies for individuals to choose their own values and life styles also lead to tensions between individual and social ideas about what is worthwhile and bring into sharp focus the problems of educating young people to be autonomous. Indeed, as we shall show in this chapter, there is still a great deal of confusion about what the claim that individual autonomy is an educational aim actually amounts to.

In the final three chapters, we look at three highly specific issues. The first of these concerns preparation for work. Economic efficiency is thought to be central to the success of the liberal democracies and engagement in paid employment is both an aspiration of and a requirement for the overwhelming majority of people in such societies. But how is the wish for self-fulfilment to be reconciled with the demands of economic efficiency? Can the two be reconciled? Chapter 8 discusses these issues, which have not always received the attention that they are due in philosophy of education, although they have, for some time, preoccupied policy-makers. In Chapter 9 we look at one of the most striking educational results of the spread of free markets and free market ideology, namely, the belief that individual aspirations, educational efficiency and fairness can be achieved through the application of market disciplines to education. In Chapter 10 we come back to the central issue that we started with, namely, competing conceptions of education and address the issue of how liberal societies can successfully accommodate, within a common system of preparation for life, the differing aspirations of ethnically, culturally and religiously diverse groups.

This book, then, is an attempt to show how philosophy of education has a very important contribution to make to our understanding of the formation of educational policy. At the same time, we try to show how philosophy of education without political and policy engagement is a diminished discipline. We have written the book so as to appeal to those without a previous philosophical background, who nevertheless wish to gain some understanding of fundamental policy issues underlying contemporary educational practice. We have provided an outline paragraph at the beginning of each chapter in order to allow people to skip sections if they wish. In addition, each chapter ends with questions for discussion and suggestions for further reading, so that particular issues can be explored in greater depth, either individually or in the context of class and seminar discussions.

Chapter 1

Values, aims and society

This chapter introduces the framework through which we will discuss the central issues in education. We begin with a discussion of the importance of values in society and go on to examine how societies can deal with different and conflicting values. Education is introduced as central to the concerns of a plural society as it is concerned with the preparation for adult life of new generations. What values should then inform education? The chapter goes on to discuss the role of values in an education system and the role of the school system in promoting them. The issue of how potentially conflicting aims can be addressed in education is then considered. We then go on to consider these questions in the context of post-compulsory, in particular, vocational education, pointing out the relationship between worthwhile lives, paid employment and education. Finally, we take an overview of three broad approaches to the development of educational policy in a liberal plural society: elitism, democracy and the use of markets.

Values in education

Values are an essential part of what people think makes their lives worthwhile. Individuals, groups or whole societies can hold them. They take the form of beliefs and attitudes, which can usually be spelled out. One's moral and religious beliefs, together with other beliefs about the kinds of things that make life worthwhile, such as friendship, satisfaction at work, family life, love of one's country, all constitute our values. Different groups may share some values, but may also differ in some. Sometimes these values may be incompatible. One cannot, for example, believe in religious freedom and hold that only one form of religion is to be permitted.

But we cannot ask people to give up what they believe makes life worth living, since these beliefs constitute part of their own identity, they make people what they are, through shaping their lives. But if people cannot give up their values, how can they live with those who hold contradictory values? How can religious believers, for example, live with atheists? One possibility is that they cannot. In this case, they either fight or agree to live apart. Another possibility is that they try to find common ground on those parts of their different beliefs that they do not mind implementing and keep private those parts of their beliefs that they cannot agree should be part of public policy. For example, atheists might suggest that religious people should be able to have optional religious services for their own children at schools that are, in other respects, non-religious. Religious believers might suggest that atheists have separate, non-religious schools. They might arrive at a compromise by agreeing to set up both kinds of school, leaving it up to parents which they send their children to. Education policy issues cannot be appreciated without understanding the central role that values play in education. But if it is difficult to reconcile different sets of values, then it is also difficult to construct education policies based on such attempts at reconciliation.

Education is a preparation for life

The concept of education refers to the human activity of preparation for life. It primarily concerns children and young people, but since one can be prepared for different phases of life, it also concerns adults who wish to re-orient the direction of their lives. However, to say that education is concerned with preparation for life is to give the concept very little content. First, there are different aspects of life, for example, work, leisure and family. Second, different individuals and groups will have different views about what are the most valuable aspects of life. What they think is valuable about an aspect of life is closely connected with the values that they hold. For example, someone who values family life may do so for, among other reasons, because they believe that the intimacy, interdependence and spontaneity of family life are essential constituents of a worthwhile existence. It is, however, particularly useful to distinguish between three aspects of the preparation for life. These are: liberal, civic and vocational. The *liberal* aspect of education concerns the preparation of someone as a person with their own potential in life, able to appreciate the culture of the community into which they are growing up and to make choices about the direction in which they wish their life to go. The *civic* aspect involves people as citizens of their society, who vote, take part in politics, voluntary or charitable activities. The *vocational* aspect involves people as agents of economic activity, for instance, as a paid employee, or as self-employed.

It is hardly surprising that there are also different views concerning the kind of individual, civic or vocational education that people should receive. The ways in which different aspects of education are played out yield different *conceptions* of education. Conceptions of education differ from the concept of education in the following way. The concept of education refers to preparation for life. A particular conception of education, however, refers to a particular kind of preparation for life. We would expect conceptions of education to be far richer in content and in what they prescribe than the concept of education itself. How different conceptions of education are related to the culture of the society and how they are put into effect in the *curriculum* will be one of the topics of Chapter 2.

One of the issues that immediately arises when a conception of education is developed is that differences within a society about what is a worthwhile preparation for life begin to emerge. Some, for example, might think that vocational preparation is unimportant, while others think that it is all-important, to the exclusion of practically anything else. To make matters more complicated, some groups within a society may favour a particular conception of education for themselves and a different one for other people. Finally, particular conceptions of education almost always reflect the values of the groups or individuals putting them forward. Beliefs about what constitutes a worthwhile life inevitably affect views about what is the most suitable preparation for a worthwhile life. When these values are wholly or partially incompatible with each other, then the question about *which* conception of education a society needs to articulate, can be difficult to resolve. We should note that individual people often belong to groups which have apparently opposing interests. Parents, for example, may be torn between a desire for more *vocational* education to develop the economy and a desire for a *liberal* education for their own child.

Someone who thinks that *equality* is the most important value will have a particular conception of education in mind for developing the maximum amount of equality. On the other hand, someone who attaches most importance to the value of *liberty* will seek to develop a conception of education that maximises liberty. The problem then, as many have observed, is that one cannot pursue the maximum degree of liberty and at the same time pursue the maximum degree of equality, since increasing equality may mean restricting someone's liberty to become, say, richer than other people. To take another example, someone may think that the most valuable kind of life involves leisured contemplation, while someone else may think that only a life spent in useful employment is valuable. Once again, it is difficult to see how one can seriously pursue both these goals for the same individual at the same time.

It would be easy to construct an ideal model of how such issues are settled in a democratic society. One would expect, for example, that different interest groups would attempt to find common ground. They would seek to establish where conflicts arise in relation to the same individual (e.g. as both parent and employee) with a view to establishing priorities and, where this is not possible, to seek compromises about which values were to be implemented and to what degree. The history of the development of state education systems suggests that a very different sort of process has occurred in many cases. First, because modern education systems were not usually set up under completely democratic conditions and, second, because it is at least arguable that democratic government is a government by an elite or competing elites, rather than depending on genuine popular debate (Green 1990; Schumpeter 1976). The United States is, perhaps, the closest example one can find of a society that set up its education system as a result of democratic debate and action. Elsewhere, in, for example,

Prussia and France, the education system was designed and set up by political elites concerned to develop their respective countries into modern industrial powers. In England and Wales, the elites, suspicious about state action, enshrined the traditional education of the gentry as the preferred form of education for the few relatively well-off members of the population, and a system of basic literacy and numeracy for the mass of people, in line with the suggestions of the political economist, Adam Smith (1776). It is arguable therefore, that one is likely to get a 'default norm' or a solution that goes with the grain of the influence and wishes of politically dominant elites rather than reflecting the priorities of the rest of the population. The arguable persistence of default norms into the democratic era suggests a continuing elitist pattern of policy-making.

Aims of education

The relationship between the values on which an education system is built and its aims is very close. This is hardly surprising, since the aims express the values. It is important to realise that an education system can have aims even when these are not formally codified. Just as one can infer someone's intentions by what they do over a period of time, often in spite of what they *claim* that they are doing, so one can infer the aims of an education system by the way in which it is operated over a period of time, whether or not it has explicit aims. Sometimes explicit aims will be a useful guide to what the system is trying to do, sometimes they will not be helpful. In those cases where there are no explicit aims, one has to look at the conduct of the system and interpret that conduct in terms of the preferences of the elites that have most influence over it.

Schools

The British education system is a good case in point. Until 1999 it had no explicitly formulated aims. It has been possible, however, to see from the beginning what its main purposes were. These were: to provide a basic mass education for the future working population, one that would combine basic literacy and numeracy with a supportive attitude to the existing social and political order (Green 1990). Those destined for higher levels of work had access to the grammar schools, which provided a variant of the traditional education of the gentry as a foundation for entry into higher education and occupations that required more than an absolutely basic level of literacy and numeracy. Finally, a small sector of secondary education was deliberately isolated from the mass education system. This 'public school' system had, as its aims, the maintenance of a political elite with the skills, attitudes and character to run the British Empire. It could be maintained that the English education system had quite clear aims that related to the development of the society as a whole and that it allowed for *liberal* aims for those few who were fortunate enough to receive a public or grammar school education. Even this latter claim needs to be treated with some caution, as there is considerable evidence that the most common type of public school education was designed precisely to stamp out individuality and to mould the type of character who could function instinctively as a member of a ruling class, as the first priority, and as a member of a leisured ruling elite secondarily. Curiously, this system also allowed for the development of 'rebels', capable of carrying out special tasks for the Empire (see, for example, the description by Rudyard Kipling in his public school story, *Stalky and Co*). Strictly speaking, liberal education in this system was something largely enjoyed by those fortunate enough to gain entry to higher education.

This perhaps makes it clearer why some societies might be reluctant to be too explicit about the aims according to which they operated their education systems. The English system, rigidly hierarchical and exclusionary as it was, together with a very strong commitment to racial superiority and the dominance of other 'lesser' peoples, was understandably reluctant to advertise what it was about.

Problems with formulating aims

If, as we saw, different groups within a society have different values, then it is not always clear how those values are going to be realised in any particular education system. The problem is most acute when values are incompatible with each other. Sometimes the problem can be avoided through the adoption of 'thin' values that express the common content of two otherwise conflicting systems of belief. For example, moral injunctions and virtues common to both Christians and Muslims could constitute a common set of values, in virtue of the partially overlapping character of the two systems of belief. This common set of values could then form the basis for a set of aims of moral education that both Christians and Muslims could agree to.

However, the proposed solution does not show how to deal with non-overlapping beliefs, for example, concerning sexual morality. The problem is made worse when we consider that a society may consist of further groups whose values may not overlap at all with those of others. The threat arises that there may be insufficient consensus in the society about values to allow for *any* common set of aims. There is a possible solution to this problem. First, one may abandon any attempt to put moral values in the curriculum, apart from those that do have an overlapping consensus. The aims of education directly relevant to morality would be those allowing procedures for settling differences, such as cultivation of the virtue of tolerance and the ability to compromise (Gray 1995). The remainder of educational aims would be made up of relatively innocuous aspirations, for example, literacy and numeracy, the cultivation of conscientious citizens and workers, and so on.

The danger, however, is that such a statement of aims would please no one and be of little practical use in the construction of the curriculum. Another solution would be to construct a thin set of common aims to apply to all schools, but allow individual schools to cater for more restricted common sets of values. There would thus be Catholic, Jewish and Muslim schools as well as common schools. One solution to these problems, favoured by many liberal thinkers, is that the only schools supported by the state should be secular (non-religious) schools, open to all. Some would maintain that only such schools should be legal. This thinking adopts the following lines. One of the main aims of education should be *autonomy*, or the ability to choose the direction of one's life. In order to be able to do this, one should not have one's choices predetermined at an age when one is not yet ready to make such choices. To educate someone into a religious value system would be to predetermine their choices. Predetermined choices preclude autonomy. But autonomy is the principal aim of the education system. Therefore, religious schools contradict the aims of the school curriculum. Therefore they should not be allowed.

This is the argument against religious schools. What is the argument in favour of secular common schools? It goes something like this. For someone to become autonomous they must be presented with a range of meaningful life-choices and must have the rational capacity to make a choice that suits their interests, values and abilities. It follows that they should not, in the period when they are not yet capable of autonomy, be brought up into a life that they can only with difficulty abandon later. They should, therefore, receive adequate information about the range of possible lives available to them and they should also develop the critical capacity to assess each of these in the light of their values, interests and abilities. Only in these conditions will they be able to make an unconstrained choice. Therefore, the state school should have as its aims the provision of enough information with which students can make a choice, and the development of powers of critical rationality so that these students are capable of making such a choice. Consideration of these issues in greater detail leads us on to the nature of the learning that takes place in schools and colleges and to the issue of whether or not it is possible to teach in a way that develops, rather than stifles, autonomy. This complex range of issues will receive more attention in Chapters 3 and 4.

The broader policy issues of the values and aims required to fill out different conceptions of education will concern us in more detail in Chapters 6 and 7, but some brief points are relevant here. First, the assumption of the liberal argument is that secular liberalism itself is not subject to the criticisms it levels against religious forms of upbringing. In other words, it assumes that secular liberalism is a way of life and a system of values that does not constrain later choice. This claim can itself be disputed. If, for example, it could be shown that a secular liberal upbringing made it difficult to autonomously choose certain worthwhile ways of living, then one of its central claims would be undermined. Yet some have argued that a secular liberal upbringing makes it very difficult to autonomously choose to lead a religious life. Secular liberalism also makes the assumption that autonomy is the supreme value to which individuals should aspire. Not everyone will agree with this. Some religiously minded educators would suggest, for example, that it is far more important to be pious and good than it is to be free to determine the course of one's life. We think that there is a liberal reply to this move, which we explore in Chapter 10.

Compulsory and non-compulsory phases of education

It is easy to forget that an important part of education for many people in developed countries takes place after they have left compulsory schooling. Much of this education, particularly in the 'higher' or university and college sector, is liberal, designed primarily to promote personal development and secondarily to develop workplace skills and the economic strength of the country. But a lot of it is explicitly designed to develop the ability to acquire workplace skills and knowledge with a view to preparing people for the labour market. It is important to remember that historically the state intervened in education and set up public education systems in Europe and other parts of the world not just to develop its citizens but also to develop the skills and knowledge considered to be essential to economic development (Green 1990). Philosophers often neglect this area of education but it is extremely important in a broader policy context and raises difficult problems for educators, as it obliges them to engage with the aims of economic activity, as well as with the aims of education. Let us explain.

There is a relationship between how a country runs its education system and the way it runs its economy. But what exactly is the nature of this relationship? We have already indicated that the aims of education are important in determining how an education system is run. Is the same true of a country's economy? This may seem an odd question since it seems obvious that economies exist so that goods and services are produced which people can then use or consume. But, it is in a sense obvious that education is about preparing young people for life. This does not stop philosophers and policy-makers arguing about the aims of education. The reason why is that 'preparation for life' is a very non-specific educational aim. Some might argue that the most important part of life that people should be prepared for is individual self-fulfilment, others might argue for civic participation, and others for paid work. Suppose one were to say that one of the aims of education was to develop a strong economy. This seems clear enough until one asks what a strong economy looks like. There seem to be a number of possible answers. One could say that a strong economy allowed a country to exist on its own resources, or that it allowed a country to become militarily and politically strong or that it was one in which many goods and services were traded and produced. So there are different possible answers to this question. However, even if the answer was to do with the trading of goods and services, there might still be a question as to *what* kinds of goods and services a country might decide to concentrate on. It is important to realise that this is not just a technical question for economists, but concerns the nature of the way of life that the people of that country are able to lead.

Post-compulsory education thus raises a new set of problems for educational aims. In fact, it is not possible to settle on educational aims without having a view of economic aims. If one believes that the aim of economic activity should be to provide employment for workers and profits for businesses, without any view about whether the market that those enterprises should occupy should be high-value or low-value, then vocational education will most likely be a form of *training* tailored to the short-term needs of the market (see Chapter 8). In such a system there will be little room for most people to develop through their work. Liberal aims, if there are any for the ordinary worker, will be pursued outside work. On the other hand, if a society takes the view that it wishes to develop a high-specification, high-skilled economy, this has important consequences both for how it influences the behaviour of enterprises and for how it shapes the school and the post-compulsory education system to achieve its goals. More radically still, a society might take the view that high-skilled work goes some way to providing the conditions for the achievement of personal satisfaction and even a degree of self-government through work. In this case, both *liberal* and *civic* aims could be pursued through the vocational education system.

Into the mix of values that a society must consider when developing the aims of its education system will come values relating to the aims of economic activity. Once again, different groups and individuals may have opposing views about what these should be.

Conclusion

We can now see how complex the setting up and running of an education system is and how difficult are the problems of planning and running it to the satisfaction of widely different interest groups within society. We wish to conclude with some thoughts on various ways in which these difficulties can be managed and the alternative paths which different solutions adopted are likely to lead to. The most obvious solution to these problems is what we call an 'elitist' one. In this case, the political elite in a society decides what the priorities are that the society should adopt and puts them into effect. The growth of the education systems in Prussia and France in the nineteenth century reflects this model. Although in these cases, the elitist model was put into effect by authoritarian (i.e. non-democratic) governments, elitism is not the sole preserve of authoritarian regimes. Indeed, elites can exist within a variety of different political systems, including *oligarchies*, one form of which is where a ruling elite governs either through election via a limited franchise, such as existed in the UK in the eighteenth and nineteenth centuries. Indeed, some political theorists have considered that modern democracies are in fact modes of competition between rival elites (Schumpeter 1958).

While elitism often gives rise to fairly clear and decisive conclusions, it does not always do so. An example is England and Wales in the nineteenth century. The ideology of the ruling elite was strongly against state intervention within either the economy or the wider society and consequently there was, for a long time, great reluctance to undertake the setting up of a state education system. When it eventually was created from the 1870s onwards, it incorporated elements of the older charitable system. Furthermore, the society took the view that economic development was not really the business of the state and neglected the vocational aspect of education (Green 1990). Elites are likely to impose their own priorities on the educational systems of their societies. Even when they are enlightened and far-sighted, there is a risk that important interest groups and important aspects of education will suffer from relative neglect.

An alternative, the democratic solution, may look like a variant of the elitist solution, for reasons that we have already seen. However, it may also, while catering for the perceived interests of the majority of voters, neglect those of many others. Thus while the development of the US education system broadly followed the democratic path of development, it arguably did so at a cost. This cost included the institutionalising of racial bigotry and educational segregation in some parts of the USA and, arguably, the development of a secondary educational system that reflected the diversity of the society by lowering educational standards in order to accommodate everyone comfortably. The general agreement to develop a secular educational system, enshrined in the Constitution, also left many parents unhappy. A general problem with democratic solutions which are not mediated by elitism can be stated as follows. Democratic electorates inevitably have limited perspectives and are more easily swayed by short-term rather than by long-term considerations. They have limited knowledge of the alternatives and are readily moved by demagogy and the fashion of the moment. Last but not least, there is the ever-present danger of the 'tyranny of the majority'. This arises when the majority of the electorate imposes a solution on minorities who disagree with them. For example, the majority of secular-minded parents might decide to outlaw state-funded religious schools against the wishes of a minority of the population.

The final and currently fashionable answer to these problems is the creation of an *educational market*. This solution involves the use of an economic mechanism in order to reconcile the preferences of different groups. In a market solution, the state gives up its right to plan and control the educational system. Instead, the various consumers of education have the right to the resources to set up and create the kind of system that suits them and their children best. We will look in detail at the philosophical and policy issues surrounding market systems in Chapter 9. They have clear and obvious advantages. The first of these, and by far the strongest, is that they promise to resolve the problem of multiple and irreconcilable interests and points of view within a society concerning the aims of the education system and the particular conception of education that it should adopt.

Put briefly, the solution is to allow as many conceptions of education to develop as there are demands for them. A conception of education will live or die by its popularity. If people adhere to a particular conception, then they will pay for it. If not, then they will not. A second claimed advantage is that the inefficiency associated with the state will be replaced by the efficiency associated with private sector provision. Finally, a market system will be flexible and quick to respond to changes in demand. It is only fair to say that there are disadvantages, as well as advantages to a market system and we will conclude this chapter by briefly mentioning these. The first is that the interests of the state or the society as a whole are not taken account of. As we argued above, this is important. Second, it assumes that the consumers (who are, in the case of children, their parents) are knowledgeable, committed and responsible enough to make the right decision. Finally, it is arguable that markets are able to provide solutions to problems that intrinsically require co-operation directed by a central body.

One important aspect of the provision of education is that of *accountability*, or the question of whether and how an education system can show that it has been effective in meeting its aims. This question implies that there are some criteria against which performance can be assessed and this in turn implies that there are *standards* against which *performance* can be measured. Not everyone believes that accountability is a requirement of public education systems and some market theorists think that evidence of demand is a sufficient criterion of effectiveness. Controversies surrounding these issues will be discussed in Chapter 5.

Enough has been said in this chapter to indicate the richness and complexity of the philosophical issues surrounding the creation and evaluation of educational policy. The rest of the book will explore particular issues in more detail.

Questions for further discussion

1   Give an example of a value that you hold. How might it conflict with someone else's value on the same topic?
2   Can education accommodate conflicting values? If so, how?
3   What are the main advantages and disadvantages of making educational aims explicit?
4   If education prepares us for adult life, how is it possible to be educated beyond the school-leaving age?
5   Should education policy be established by those who know best?

Further reading

For a discussion of the elite theory of democracy, see Joseph Schumpeter, *Capitalism, Socialism and Democracy* (London, Routledge, 1976). Adam Smith's views on education can be found in *The Wealth of Nations*, Book V, Part II, Article III (Indianapolis, Liberty Fund, 1981).

Andy Green's, *Education and State Formation* (London, Macmillan, 1990), illustrates how politically dominant views on education can shape the way in which a society orders its education system.

David Ashton and Francis Green's *Education, Training and the Global Economy* (Cheltenham, Edward Elgar, 1996) is a good account of the relationship between education systems and economic performance.

For a defence of the market as an allocator of educational resources, see James Tooley, *Reclaiming Education* (London, Cassell, 2000). For an excellent survey of debates concerning liberalism and the accommodation of differing views on how life should be lived, see Stephen Mulhall and Adam Swift, *Liberals and Communitarians* (Oxford, Blackwell, 1996).

Chapter 2

Culture and the curriculum

In this chapter, the concept of culture is examined and it is argued that, for educational purposes, 'culture' needs to be interpreted to mean 'the best that has been thought and done'. 'Curriculum' is defined and it is shown how it is concerned with culture and with the aims of education. The chapter goes on to look at the desirability or otherwise of national curricula and argues that they are desirable in certain circumstances. Objections are considered and dismissed. The English National Curriculum is considered in detail as a case study of the implementation of a national curriculum and its strong and weak points are assessed.

The roles of schooling

Schools are institutions to which, in our society, we delegate the responsibility for a large part of the education of our children. We do so because most of us are convinced that parents have neither the time, expertise, social contacts and, perhaps, inclination to provide the education that we require for children in their own homes. But because our expectations with regard to education are many and various, it will necessarily be the case that we expect schools to fulfil several different roles. So, for instance, it is difficult to see how schools could fulfil any functions at all unless they – or the educational authorities which control them – assumed a basic child-minding function. That is, some effort has to be made so that children attend school and their basic physical well-being is catered for when they attend. We also expect schools to contribute to the socialisation and moral education of our children, not necessarily by having lessons in good manners or the evils of bullying and racism, but by emphasising in all they do that certain types of actions and attitudes are to be encouraged and others are to be discouraged. Such roles are always important and, at some stages of schooling, may provide the main justification for schooling. So, for instance, this government has pledged that it will ensure that nursery education is available for all children. The long-term evidence for the academic benefit of such schooling is non-existent, such evidence in terms of social or moral learning is inconclusive,[1] but its benefits as a child-minding exercise which frees parents, especially mothers, for employment may be enough to justify the exercise. However, important as such things may be, most of us, we suspect, would not see them as a significant justification for the vast machinery and expense of schooling within our society. For such justification we have to look elsewhere. And the place to look, we will argue, is at the transmission of culture.

The varieties of culture and questions of choice

All societies seek to pass on those things they deem to be culturally valuable. In simple societies, e.g. those where life revolves around hunting and gathering, initiation into these cultural values may be relatively informal, e.g. by children accompanying adults on hunting parties, or relatively quick, e.g. through initiation ceremonies at the onset of adulthood. In our enormously complex society such initiation demands the formal, institutional and long-term practices we typically associate with schooling. And within our schools the main engine for the delivery of such cultural values will be the curriculum. Thus, the main aim of education and therefore schooling will be cultural transmission. And the main vehicle for the delivery of such cultural values will be that set of planned and prescribed activities which deliberately seek to foster the knowledge, skills and attitudes associated with such values. This is what we call the 'curriculum', which consists of what *should* go on in schools.

It is important at this stage of the argument to emphasise three things. First, that the part of education made up of compulsory schooling will only constitute an initiation into such cultural values. The full pursuit of such values is a life-long task. So, for instance, if paid employment is to be culturally valued, as it is in our society, we would expect some reference to this during the period of compulsory schooling. However, we would not expect such schooling to be totally dominated by this value. Second, the values in question are of such a nature that a large part of schooling, e.g. the primary phase, will be concerned with a grounding in these skills which are necessary for an engagement with such values, i.e. it will be an introduction to an introduction. Thus, one cannot engage with history, literature or science unless one can read, write and count. And, finally, such a transmission of values is not merely an imposition of our values upon a passive new generation but rather an attempt by us to give that generation a choice with the cultural goods we have to offer.

Having suggested an aim for education, we now have to give some substance to that suggestion and the ways in which such an aim becomes instantiated within a curriculum. The notion that education is the transmitter of our cultural values is not a new one. It goes back, at least, to the work of Matthew Arnold and especially his *Culture and Anarchy* written at the end of the 1860s (Arnold [1869] 1935). While much of Arnold's text is still salutary reading, especially, for instance, his insistence that culture is made up of more than one tradition and that what we should expect of education is a full, critical engagement with such culture, much of what he says is extremely general. He does not, for instance, address the particular questions of how we identify the cultural values we wish to transmit and how we exemplify these within a curriculum. So, ground-clearing work still has to be done.[2]

Our ideas of culture usually take one of three forms. The first, and most general of these is what we might call the sociological or anthropological conception of culture. Culture here is defined as:

All the beliefs and practices of a given group or society.

In this sense, we might talk of English or Spartan culture and almost anything that went on within such groups – excepting things such as biological and physical processes which transcend societal boundaries – would be relevant to such usage. Now it is obviously the case that any education that goes on within a given society must depend upon the culture of that society in this sense of the word. However, this sense is both too broad and too value-neutral to be much good when deciding the basis of our education system. Too broad: in that institutional education by its limited nature cannot hope to pass on everything that goes on in a culture. Too value-neutral: in that because we have to select cultural items for inclusion within education and seek some justification for that selection, we will tend to leave out items which we think that schools cannot effectively pass on, e.g. the pleasures of family life; and those things we do not wish schools to pass on. In this latter category will be those parts of our culture which we regard as immoral, e.g. sexism and racism, but also those parts which we regard as inherently trivial or banal. No education system which is concerned with what is valuable can engage with the trivial, and the banal we can leave to mechanisms outside our schools.

This exclusion of the nasty, trivial and banal pushes us towards our second definition of culture:

The intellectual and artistic beliefs of a given group or society.

But even this more narrow definition does not solve our problems of choice. There will be still too much here for any education system limited to a few hours a day for eleven or thirteen years of a person's life to deal with. (And the extra years of tertiary education will not alter this point.) But also, if we treat the 'intellectual' and 'artistic' categories in their widest, descriptive sense, e.g. any series of thoughts, and attempts at writing, painting or music, any engagement with the past, then we run into the same problem we had with our first definition. For it is manifestly the case that our intellectual and artistic lives – in this wide sense – also include much that is trivial, banal and nasty. This is merely to say that much of thought and art of any age is either bad in its own terms or bad because we think it immoral. It is often both instructive and interesting to study bad examples of thought and art, e.g. the phrenology craze of the nineteenth century; or the work of an extremely minor poet, but if we are sincerely concerned with the passing on of what is culturally valuable, then the instruction and the interest here depend upon placing these within a context of good examples.

This pushes us towards our – and Arnold's – third definition of culture. Culture in this sense is:

> The best intellectual and artistic beliefs and practices of a given group of people or society.

Arnold called this 'the best that has been thought and known' (ibid., p. 6). Perhaps better, if we do not want to assimilate all artistic production to the intellect, is the best that has been thought and done. This idea of the role and content of education is not a popular one (although we think it is presupposed by much contemporary debate concerning education). However, before we go on to try to deal with objections to this conception of education, let us look at some of the things it has to offer. First, if we want students in our schools and universities to critically engage with some of the best examples taken from our cultural traditions, then this must involve the depth of understanding which has been thought to characterise education as such.[3] Simply learning a list of the battles of the Duke of Wellington does not constitute a critical engagement with history. Second, because of the scope and complexity of our culture – but not, perhaps, all cultures – an education devoted to such things will have the type of breadth which, again, has been thought to be essential in any proper educational enterprise (Peters 1966).

Third, if in educating our children we want both to expose them to the types of thing we think valuable and, in doing so, enable them to function and flourish within our society after their education has finished, then the type of education proposed seems ideally suited to doing both things.[4] This point may be put another way. It is sometimes assumed that a key feature of education must be that it is relevant to those being educated. But 'relevance' is a very slippery concept because of its relational nature. If something is relevant it has to be relevant for someone and in relation to some purpose that person has or might have. And it is all too easy to simply make assumptions concerning such persons and purposes. To observe, for instance, that home economics is a relevant thing to teach girls because, in being girls, the home will be the focus of their future interests. But such assumptions both about girls' nature and their future interests seem obviously unwarranted. If we really wish our education system to offer choices to those being educated – both within schools and after school – then we must avoid such assumptions. The most that we can assume is that there is a range of things that people might be interested in throughout and after their education. Given that this is so, and given that the education we propose contains those things which we find culturally valuable, then it also seems obviously relevant given this limited assumption.

Fourth, although we have talked about such an education being an initiation into the values of *our* culture, it is fairly clear that it will quickly take us beyond the merely parochial. So, for instance, to be introduced to mathematics and science is not, and could not be, to be simply introduced to British mathematics and science, for there are, in a real sense, no such things. There are certainly British painters and composers but our musical and visual culture goes far beyond them. We have a rich literary tradition but it exists within the contexts of wider traditions and can only properly be understood within such contexts. This being said, there may be incidental benefits which accrue from studying the relatively familiar. So, for all we can tell, it is perfectly possible to become competent in the study of, say, History by focussing on the history of China. However, for most of us, the inaccessibility of the source material, both in terms of distance and language, and the fact that when we walk our streets we cannot see the effects of the Han dynasty but we can of the Western Classical tradition and of the Industrial Revolution, seem to tell against this as an initiation into history.

Finally, but importantly, if we are through education initiating pupils into the best that has been thought and done, then this is, in a way, self-justifying. Given any choice between types of thing or activity, e.g. which wine to choose on the menu, which football match to watch, which book or poem to read, which music to listen to, then to be told that a particular example or set of examples is the best of the bunch is to be given a reason to choose that one or that set. Certainly, if given such a choice, we would be either insulted or mystified to be offered the second best or the worst of the type. There may be reasons for such an offer – the best wine may be overpriced and the best poem too difficult for us at this stage of our literary career – but the very fact that such reasons have to be made in this case, but not when we are directed to the best, makes our point exactly. And this also leads us nicely onto the first objection that might be made concerning such a curriculum.

Choosing the best

Such an objection, crudely put, is that there are no ways to select the best within the types of thing we are dealing with; that we have no criteria whereby we can rank such things in order of value. Such a sceptical claim is both wide ranging and may be difficult to refute in detail (see Gingell and Brandon 2000, Chapter 3). However, even if we do not have the space for such a refutation here, we can make some general points which show that the sceptical position is unlikely to be true.

The first point to make is that, in talking about the best that has been thought and done, we are not concerned with providing a total, lexical order of value. So whether we are talking about science, literature, history or any other type of thing which might occur within a curriculum, we do not assume that such subjects or items can be assigned a precise place like football teams at the end of the season in the Football League. Our claim is more modest than this. It is that given such categories, there are ways of telling what things fit into the category and what things do not, e.g. what is science and what is non-science, and within the categories it is possible to see that some items are better than others, e.g. that, as far as plays are concerned, *Hamlet* is more interesting than *The Spanish Tragedy*. Both these modest claims are, at times, easily demonstrable. So, for instance, to take a case within the news at the moment, if it is claimed that the account of creation of the world offered in the Bible is a scientific hypothesis on a par with Darwin's theory of evolution, it is fairly easy to show that because of its reliance on sacred texts, its attitude to historical and cultural scholarship and the ways it deals with evidence from the natural world, that it is not an alternative scientific account to Darwin but rather an anti-scientific rejection of Darwin. If this is so, then to allow such an account on a science syllabus is to make such a syllabus incoherent (ibid., pp. 49–52).

As far as the notion of ranking within the categories goes, it seems widely accepted within those groups of people who professionally deal with such matters, e.g. professors and lecturers of literature, art history, music (and such disciplines as history, sociology and philosophy) that such a ranking, in our modest sense, is possible, that it is, in all these areas, possible to talk of a canon of material worth studying. Of course there always are, and should be, arguments about the borders of such canons, e.g. should Aphra Benn or Margaret Atwood be included in the literary canon? Is the winner of the latest Turner Prize for art a good artist or someone decided by fashion? Such arguments should not surprise anyone who does not, completely unrealistically, suppose that the boundaries of the canons will be absolutely precise and clearly discernible. But such boundary disputes simply emphasise the fact that it is the extent rather than the existence of the canon that is in question. We may find it hard to say where, on a spectrum, red ends and yellow begins but this does not mean we cannot identify clear cases of red and yellow.

Admittedly, selecting our curriculum material from the upper reaches of our intellectual and artistic enterprises is elitist but, for the reasons given above, we do not think that this is objectionable. It may offend those to whom any value distinctions are obnoxious but such people are both unreasonable and in the minority (see below and also Gingell and Brandon 2000, Chapter 3). But the suggestions are also elitist in another sense which we also think is innocent. If our curriculum material is to come from our intellectual and artistic traditions, then it will have to be chosen by those who know about such traditions. As people with such expertise are typically found in those institutions whose business is the study of such traditions, e.g. universities, such experts will typically decide – again probably after some argument – what is to count as an example of the tradition in question, e.g. what is to count as science and what are to count are good examples of the tradition. And, finally, what are reasonable ways of approaching such good examples? This is to say nothing more than that scientists are the best people to decide upon the matter and manner of studying science; literary critics are the best people to advise on the matter and manner of the study of literature, etc.

To the idea that this hands over curriculum choice to unrepresentative experts (see Wolff 1992) we have two replies. First, if you seek reasoned choice in such areas, then you must go to those people who, from experience and training, are capable of making such choices. To ask the ignorant and indifferent to select material for, say, the study of English literature would be absurd. Second, and most importantly, such choices must be presented and defended in public debate. In trying to select curriculum material for our children, i.e. all the children of the country, we have to be in a position where we can endorse – or reject – such choices. We can only do this if the choices and the reasons behind them are matters of public debate.

Although our suggestions are elitist in these unobjectionable ways, they are certainly not elitist in ways that would be very objectionable. So, for instance, this is *not* a curriculum for *some* of our children. It does not assume – as some have assumed in the past – that only a favoured few can benefit from the types of material which will be on offer (see Bantock 1971; Barrow 1993). Until very recently popular theories in psychology and social psychology seemed to show that because of, say, variations of intelligence or variations in verbal skill only some children were capable of educational success (see Eysenck 1973; Bernstein 1973). Such theories have been the subject of comprehensive and detailed attacks (see Winch 1990). And such attacks have, we think, been completely successful. Probably the most successful indicator of educational success is social class. Working-class children are less likely, for instance, to go to university than their middle-class counterparts. However, a significant proportion of working-class children do go on to tertiary education. Given that this is the case and, given any group of working-class children, the only fair procedure is to assume that these children are capable of educational success and to try to ensure, as far as possible, that they attain such success. To make any other assumption is to engage in blatantly begging the question and thereby ensuring a particularly nasty self-fulfilling prophecy. A common curriculum provided for all is a very recent innovation in this country. Even compulsory secondary education is still within its experimental phase. (One of the authors of this book was part of the first generation to be born who could expect such an education.) Such measures are the proper indicators of an educational system concerned with social justice and the only way in which we can realistically investigate the educational capabilities of our children. Until such an investigation is complete – and, given the variable quality of educational provision at the moment, this will not be for a very long time – we must assume that all children can be given the educational resources which will enable them to function and flourish within our society. That is, that our education system can and should provide a significant amount – perhaps the most significant amount – of cultural capital for all our children. The knowledge, skill and understanding given to children at school are vitally important for their ability to flourish in later life. Unless it can be shown that we should give different amounts of these things to different children, then we must assume a basic equality of provision, which means, in this context, a basic common curriculum.

National curricula

Many countries have national curricula, or prescribed content of education for the nation's schools (e.g. France). Many do not (e.g. the United States). Some countries have recently adopted a national curriculum. England is an example of this and, because it is familiar to the authors, we will refer to it as an example of a national curriculum and use it as a case study. Bear in mind that the points that we make concerning curricula in general particularly bear on the policy implications of introducing national curricula. This means that our talk of curriculum choice has not been superseded by events. We have had successive governments dedicated to a national curriculum and we now have in place such a curriculum. But it would be a simple, and rather silly, mistake to believe because a country has a national curriculum, that this particular curriculum is the one it ought to have, i.e. that this is the *right* curriculum. Both the existence and the nature of the English National Curriculum deserve comment.

Probably the most fertile time for theories concerning the curriculum in Britain was the 1970s. During that period, commentators such as White (1973), Hirst (1974) and Barrow (1976) opened the case for a common national curriculum. It seems reasonable therefore to see the curriculum presented in the 1988 Education Reform Act as, at least partly, growing out of such arguments. However, while the types of curriculum item wanted by the above theorists were similar, there were differences of emphasis between the different theories and profound differences of justification. The National Curriculum of the 1988 Act, although influenced in spirit by these theories, seemed both in detail and justification not to be the product of any of them.

What did unite both the theorists concerned and the founders of the National Curriculum was the failure to even begin to engage with an argument against the institution of a national curriculum put forward by one of the greatest liberal thinkers of all time. John Stuart Mill in his enormously influential essay *On Liberty*, published in 1859, had this to say about such a curriculum:

> A general state education is a mere contrivance for moulding people to be exactly like one another: and as the mould in which it casts them is that which pleases the predominant power in the government, whether this be a monarch, a priesthood, an aristocracy, or the majority of the existing generation, in proportion as it is efficient and successful, it establishes a despotism over the mind leading by natural tendency to one over the body.
>
> (Mill [1859] 1968, p. 161)

But not only were the theorists who preceded the National Curriculum silent concerning this argument, they were also, largely, silent concerning the

National Curriculum itself. John White did, in 1988, produce an article: 'Two National Curricula – Baker's and Stalin's: Towards a Liberal Alternative' (White 1988), which attempted to discredit the National Curriculum by associating it with the totalitarian regime of the former Soviet Union – hence the title – and which produced one real recommendation for political and social education, which has largely been satisfied by the later institution of citizenship education. It then proceeded to make the case again for a national curriculum! That such an important piece of educational reform came into being without profound examination by philosophers of education (including the current authors) is a standing rebuke to the members of that discipline. There were later, and somewhat more adequate, responses to the National Curriculum (which we will deal with below), but we suspect that most of the work remains to be done. We have not the space to do more here than begin the debate.

Let us begin with Mill. He was surely right, in 1859, to distrust the idea of a government-directed education. Although nominally democratic, the government of the day was clearly unrepresentative of the people at large. The franchise was still severely restricted, despite the Reform Act of 1832, and Parliament was dominated by the landed classes. It was not until the twentieth century when we achieve universal – or near universal – adult suffrage that government can claim to be properly representative. But even then some of the point of Mill's distrust remains. Given the power of education itself and therefore of the government acting through education, it will always be the case that such actions are the proper object of public scrutiny.

Mill was wrong in believing that, if we can ensure that the government does not direct education, we can safely leave such direction to other bodies. The obvious candidates for such direction might be parents, educationalists, or local authorities. While such groups will, obviously, have views on education and should have ways of making such views known, there are very strong arguments against leaving them to direct education.

Parents, for instance, do not have, in general, the necessary expertise to design and see to the implementation of a curriculum. And typically they bring to educational matters beliefs and prejudices which may be inimical to education as such and detrimental to the education of their own children. So, for example, you are unlikely to be able to produce a plan for a nationally defensible programme of education for all our children, if you share the belief, which was until recently quite common, that it is a waste of time educating girls beyond the primary level. It is a salutary fact to remember in this context, that it was working-class parents in England (but not Scotland) who opposed compulsory education, and that before the raising of the leaving age until 16, it was also such parents who either allowed their children to leave at 15 before they took a public exam or demanded that they did.

The notion that educationalists should themselves determine the curriculum fares little better than the notion that it should be left to parents. Educationalists, typically, represent a particular discipline and see education from the viewpoint of that discipline. They may be committed, for instance, to the provision of science, or literature, or art history, within a curriculum but it does not necessarily follow that they are committed to an adequate overall curriculum. Indeed, it could be argued – persuasively we think – that many of the teething problems of the present National Curriculum – and especially those problems associated with the inflation of subject content – were directly and understandably the result of particular discipline groups trying to ensure that as much of their subject occurred within the curriculum despite the effect that this might have on the package as a whole which lacked overall coordination. It is also the case that in talking about a national curriculum – or any curriculum – we are talking about matters which involve educational, moral and political ideas and, whatever the particular expertise educationalists bring to their disciplines, they cannot, because no one can, be expert in the determination of such ideals.

With local authorities the case against their control of the curriculum partly reflects what is said above but is, partly, different. When local authorities did have much more influence on the curriculum of schools within their areas, i.e. before the 1988 Education Act, they exercised such influence through locally appointed educationalists who often tried to impose their ideals concerning education upon local schools. Such ideals were not the subject of local discussion or negotiation and were often badly thought through and sometimes educationally dangerous.[5] It may be the case that if we did have a tradition of vibrant and far-reaching local democracy in which educational issues were the subject of proper debate by all the interested parties, then a forceful argument could be made for local control of the curriculum. But it is not the case and therefore such an argument cannot be made.

And that, therefore, leaves the state. But not any state. Mill, in stating his opposition to a national curriculum, treats as the same, things that are, in fact, very different. There are certainly very strong arguments against letting one section of the population, e.g. a monarch, priesthood or aristocracy, impose their educational ideals, and therefore their ideals concerning the preparation for a good life, upon the rest of the population. And this is equally true if we have an education system within states whose government is dominated by one of these groups. The same arguments, however, cannot be used against the imposition of a national curriculum by the governments in a liberal democracy. The liberal element here should ensure that such a curriculum, while focussing upon the preparation for a good life that education is supposed to provide for those being educated, remains neutral as far as the content of such a life is concerned. That is to say that such an education, in so far as it is a reflection of liberalism, should attempt to enable those being educated to choose between the various versions of a good life on offer, but cannot impose any of these versions upon people or dispose the children in its schools to choose one version rather than another. This means in practice that such a curriculum must, in some way, reflect the variety of interest groups in such a society without endorsing any of them (see Chapter 10). And this in turn means that the curriculum is the subject of negotiation between such interest groups so that it can be clearly seen to reflect the common interest but nothing more. Such negotiation will never be painless – because interest groups will want more than they can have – but the results do not have to be anaemic. The key liberal values of equality, liberty and tolerance are enough, in themselves, to provide a robust framework for education.

The democratic part of this equation ensures, as far as this is possible, that such a curriculum continues to reflect the common good. Mill's general argument in *On Liberty* is that the powers of even a democratic government should be limited to those areas of life where public harm is at stake. What exactly counts as such harm is still a matter of intense debate. However, it seems fairly clear that if some children are not educated when the rest are, or if they are miseducated, then they are harmed. This being so, then education is a proper focus for government and if, as we have argued, such harm could come about should particular interest groups control the content of education, then such content should be controlled by government. Of course, democratic governments are not always wise or rational, but then this is true of any group within society and, unlike other groups, such a government may be replaced when it ceases to be wise or rational. There may be dangers of government control here, but such dangers are greatly increased if the control is elsewhere.

We said, at the beginning of this section, that the coming of our National Curriculum might serve as an illustration for the imposition of any such curriculum, either in this country or elsewhere. Given that this is so, it is instructive to look at some of the criticisms that can be aimed at such a process (see Tooley 1996, Chapter 6). First, we have argued that such a curriculum demands a democratic debate concerning its scope and limits. It might be suggested that in our particular case there was no such debate. An answer to this charge depends upon an understanding of what constitutes such a debate in a liberal democracy. Such a debate, on any proposed legislation cannot, for both practical and theoretical reasons imply that all such legislation is subject in all its detail to a vote by a national referendum. Partly because such a referendum must be a blunt instrument which cannot deal with issues of extreme complexity and, partly, because framing the terms of the question to be posed in such a referendum is a large part of the problem. So, for instance, to ask the public whether they want a national curriculum as such, is too narrow a question. To ask them whether they want one spelled out in all its detail, is far too broad. What debate involves here is not direct questioning of an electorate but rather the airing of different views in the media and specialist publications, the consultation of experts and interested parties, and the creation of mechanisms to ensure that all relevant points of view are given representation. All of these things were present in the period from 1970 to 1990 in England before the full implementation of the National Curriculum.

The second criticism that can be made of any national curriculum is that it must, by its very nature, rule out other competing visions of the curriculum.

This to a large extent must be true. After all, it is the existence of such competing visions which provide the reason for having a national curriculum in the first place. Such visions will sometimes reflect the views of particular interest groups, who wish either to carve their niche within the education system or impose their vision on everybody else. But sometimes such visions will reflect different attempts by various individuals or groups to map out a curriculum for the common good. It is exactly the role of a liberal democratic government to choose between such visions and, in this sense, such alternatives are a necessary condition for a centralised curriculum rather than an argument against it. However, this does not mean that such a curriculum must be unchangeable. Any reasonable education system must include mechanisms for critical review and possible change. And the very possibility of such changes means that we will always need competing visions of what might be in order to review the existing provision of what, in fact, is in place.

The final criticism has to do with the bureaucracy involved in a national curriculum. Here the argument is that such a bureaucracy leaves individual schools unable to react to local conditions, including some that are created by the attempt to create the curriculum in question. So, for instance, one might cite the problems that arose in the teaching of literacy and numeracy in primary schools when the National Curriculum in England was introduced. The idea here is that if schools were free of central control they would notice and react to the bad consequences of educational change in a more efficient way than is possible for a centralised bureaucracy. Obviously some parts of this argument are sound. A national curriculum, by its very nature, must involve more bureaucracy than a school-based curriculum. However, the argument, as it stands, assumes two things which if true, are only contingently so, i.e. it may be the case that these things happen, but they could be avoided. First, it assumes that individual schools must slavishly implement everything a national curriculum requires in a unified manner despite any bad consequences that may follow from such implementation. There may be national curricula like this where almost everything is a matter of centralised control. Indeed, this was one of the criticisms that was repeatedly levelled at the French National Curriculum in the first half of the twentieth century. However, not all national curricula are like this. In the present English case, through its programmes of study and attainment targets, it indicates its expectations for children's learning throughout their years of compulsory schooling, but how such expectations are met is largely left to the individual schools. This means that schools are free to design their own models for implementation and change such models if this is necessary. They are even free, although this may be frowned upon by the central authorities, to downplay some of these expectations if they think that they cannot be met without harming other aspects of the children's education. So, for instance, geography could be sacrificed to literacy. The provision of religious education provides an interesting example here. Under the Education Act of 1996, schools must provide religious education for all pupils. Many schools simply ignore this part of the Act.

The second dubious assumption in the above argument is that individual schools are quick to notice and respond to educational problems. If we look at the behaviour of primary schools with regard to, say, the teaching of reading, this assumption seems ill founded. Many such schools in the late 1980s adopted the apprenticeship or real books approach to the teaching of reading (see the influential F. Smith 1985). There is evidence to suggest that such approaches cause a decline in reading standards (Turner 1990). However, it was not such evidence which caused such schools to review their literacy policies but rather the fact that two main political parties publicly aligned themselves with a phonics approach to reading.

When the National Curriculum was introduced, there were problems concerning both its scope and its implementation. With such a major change in educational policy it would have been surprising had there not been some problems. But neither these problems, nor the other objections given above, provide a good basis for arguments against a national curriculum and, as there are good arguments in favour of such a curriculum, it is these which should take the day.

The current English National Curriculum

Having established that we should have *a* national curriculum does not, of course, establish that we should have *the* National Curriculum. It is to this issue we turn in the last part of this chapter. However, although our focus is to a large extent local, many of the issues raised can be applied to any attempt to create a national curriculum.

The National Curriculum as presently constituted is made up of twelve subject areas taught over four key stages. The subjects are: English, Mathematics, Science, Design and Technology, Information and Communication Technology, History, Geography, Modern Foreign Languages, Art and Design, Music, Physical Education, Citizenship. The key stages represent the years 5–7, 7–11, 11–14, 14–16. Of the above subjects, the first three are core subjects which have to be taught throughout all key stages. The rest are non-core foundation subjects. Of these, Design and Technology, Information and Communication Technology, and Physical Education have also to be taught throughout all stages. History, Geography, Art and Design, and Music are to be taught in the first three key stages, i.e. until age 14 years, and Modern Foreign Languages, and Citizenship are to be taught in the last two key stages, i.e. from 11 years to 16 years (although languages have now become optional at Key Stage 4). Schools also have statutory duty to provide Religious Education throughout the key stages and primary schools must have a policy for Sex Education. However, parents can withdraw their children from Religious and Sex Education lessons.

Given the above, how does this fit with what we have said about a national curriculum and its connections to liberal democratic values and our culture?

If one looks merely at the list of subjects, then these, to a large extent, do seem the type of educational areas which might provide a basis for satisfying such values and such cultural aims. (The absence of any mention of social sciences seems rather puzzling given the prominence of these within our society and their popularity as subjects for study at university.) However, one *might* make a case that such subjects are properly only studied after 16 years. (A similar case *might* also be made for Philosophy.) The detailed criticism that has been made of the National Curriculum as it stands has been directed at Modern Foreign Languages, Mathematics and History. With the first of these it has been argued (Williams, K. 2000) that we do not need them on the curriculum at all. With the other two, it is claimed (Bramall and White 2000) that the curriculum distorts their relative importance, i.e. that there is no reason to teach Mathematics beyond Key Stage 3 and every reason to teach History throughout all key stages.

None of these arguments are particularly compelling. A case could be made for regarding the teaching of Modern Foreign Languages as exemplifying a culture, very properly, looking beyond itself. With some cultures, e.g. those that speak languages which are not used on the international stage, e.g. Dutch or Catalan, such a gesture towards the outside may have profound, practical implications. With our culture, which speaks a language that has become the world language, such a gesture may be largely symbolic. But some symbols are important enough to figure within education.

With Mathematics there are strong practical reasons for continuing it throughout compulsory education, given requirements for numeracy in many areas of employment and, like Science, it represents one of the towering achievements not merely of our culture but of human culture. As for History, the concerns of Bramall and White that children might not be exposed to Modern History, could be met in Key Stage 3.

However, whatever the outcomes of these particular arguments, they may indicate a deeper problem. This is that a serious educational commitment to all twelve subjects is simply not possible especially during the last two key stages. It is impossible for all children to study all the subjects in a reasonable manner throughout their secondary education. The present National Curriculum which enables children to drop History, Geography, Art and Design, and Music in Key Stage 4 seems to imply such a conclusion. But implication may not be enough here. If it is impossible to study all subjects, then more thought has to be given to student choice in the final key stage. So, for example, an education at this stage which included History, Art and Music but with excluded Design and Technology, and Information and Communication Technology, does not, on the face of it, seem educationally absurd.

If we move from the subjects that make up the National Curriculum to the values and aims that serve – or ought to serve – as their justification, different problems occur. And here the problems are not merely those of detail but rather of basic design. When the National Curriculum was introduced in 1988 its statement of aims was perfunctory in the extreme. The new curriculum was to be:

> 'Broad, balanced and relevant' and was therefore to 'promote the spiritual, moral, cultural, mental and physical development of pupils at the school and of society' and to 'prepare such pupils for the opportunities, responsibilities and experiences of adult life'.
>
> (DES 1988)

There was no indication as to how the National Curriculum was supposed to serve these aims. Nor was there any indication given that the framers of these aims realised that breadth, balance and relevance are all relative terms. Something cannot be broad or balanced except measured against something else. To claim that something is relevant is to imply that there is someone *for whom* it is relevant and some goal *for* which it is relevant, e.g. it is relevant for someone to study Science at school if they wish to study Physics at university. Given that we were not told what the proposed curriculum was being measured against and for whom and for what it was relevant, this part of the statement of aims was empty of significant content. The next two parts were so bland as to be useless as either a guide to action or a means of curriculum assessment.

The 1999 statement of 'values, aims and purposes' for the National Curriculum sets out to remedy the vagueness seen above but, again, leaves too many questions unanswered (DfEE 1999). In the place of the original paragraph we have now three pages of values, aims and purposes. However, these are not supposed to characterise the National Curriculum but rather the school curriculum which 'comprises all learning and other experiences that each school plans for its pupils'. The National Curriculum is merely 'an important element of the school curriculum'. Such vagueness of focus is extremely unfortunate. If we are not told which of the elements of schooling are supposed to deliver which value, aim or purpose, then we can have no way of knowing whether such things are being delivered in an acceptable manner. It is no good here trying to take refuge in some kind of total package argument, e.g. we can't tell you which parts of the package deliver which outcome but you'll see when the whole is completed the outcomes will be delivered, because this means, first, that for any group of children we cannot tell whether their education is working or not until it is completed, and this is, for these children, unacceptable. Second, because we cannot tell which elements are supposed to contribute which outcome, we have no way of deciding whether such elements are going well or not.

When we move from the introduction to the values, aim and purposes to the statements of those things, we experience, compared to the 1988 version, an embarrassment of riches. So not only do we have the value of education for individual well-being and equality of opportunity but education as a contributor to 'valuing ourselves, our families and other relationships' and education as reaffirming our commitment to 'truth, justice, honesty, trust and a sense of duty'.

As far as aims go, these are twofold. The first of these is admirably brief and to the point:

Aim 1: the school curriculum should aim to provide opportunities for all pupils to learn and achieve.

(ibid., p. 10)

The spelling out of this in the next two paragraphs of the document is also clear and easily related to the curriculum. But in the third paragraph the writers go into overdrive again. We get creative and critical thinking and enabling students 'to make a difference for the better' and the school curriculum as providing an opportunity for pupils to become 'creative, innovative, enterprising and capable of leadership' (ibid., p. 11). The second aim reproduces the nebulous quality of the 1988 version. It is:

Aim 2: the school curriculum should aim to promote pupils' spiritual moral, social and cultural development and prepare all pupils for the opportunities, responsibilities and experiences of life.

(ibid., p. 11)

This is spelled out, in part, developing the pupils' awareness and understanding of the environment and securing their commitment 'to sustainable development at personal, local, national and global level'. The curriculum should also, so we are told, help pupils to form and maintain 'worthwhile and satisfying relationships based on respect for themselves and for others at home, school, work and in the community' (ibid.).

As with the statement of values, the problem here is partly one of focus. If we cannot tell which elements of schooling are supposed to fulfil which aims, then we have no way of knowing whether the elements are working or not. But it is also a problem of scope. Schooling and education may do many things, but they cannot do everything. It is not at all clear, for instance, that the school curriculum can develop pupils spiritually and morally. Nor that it can make them well-balanced, altruistic citizens with satisfying personal relationships. It may be that the ethos of schools might contribute to such things but to see these things as the aims of education threatens to seriously distort our view of education. It is surely possible, for instance, to be well educated as we currently understand it and, at the same time, neurotic, selfish and incapable of sustaining relationships. Such a person may regret their life but may be being completely unreasonable if they blame their education for their ills.

What seems to have gone wrong here is that the framers of the 1999 statement of aims, in trying to avoid the vacuity of the 1988 version, have produced a list of every aim that might conceivably be attached to education in the hope that this will silence the critics with its grandeur. But this is not what is called for. What we need – and this is not an optional extra to be tacked on to the list of subjects – is a clear, modest and realistic account of the values and aims to be realised by both schooling in general and the National Curriculum in particular, and a transparent account as to how the school and the curriculum will produce the deserved outcomes.

Conclusion

The curriculum must, by its very nature, draw upon the culture of the society for which it is a curriculum. But, if it is to be acceptable, it must do more than this. If it is to be a *worthwhile* curriculum it must involve making value choices as to what items of our culture should be included and what should be excluded. And such choices, if they are to be rational rather than arbitrary, must assume that there are objective grounds for choice. The fact that England has the National Curriculum for all its children seems to show that a large part of English educational establishment has accepted that this is the case. We have argued that there are good grounds for such a curriculum. However, we have also argued that we must see it as work in progress and not make the mistake of believing that what we have at the moment is necessarily the best that we might have.

Questions for discussion

1 Can you have a curriculum without aims for education?
2 Who should decide curriculum content?
3 'Anyone who proposes that a subject should be added to the curriculum should, at the same time, propose what should be taken out.' Comment, using a subject that you think should be on the curriculum which is not at the moment.
4 Can popular culture have any role in a curriculum dedicated to high culture?
5 Is elitism in education always a bad thing?

Further reading

Very little has recently been published on culture and the curriculum. It is worthwhile reading some earlier contributions to discussions concerning culture, for instance T.S. Eliot's *Notes Towards a Definition of Culture* (London, Faber and Faber, 1948). Assessments of Arnold's contribution to educational debate are contained in G. Sutherland (ed.), *Arnold and Education* (Harmondsworth, Penguin, 1973). A polemical introduction to culture is contained in Roger Scruton's *An Intelligent Person's Guide to Modern Culture* (London, Duckworth, 1998), G.H. Bantock's 'Towards a Theory of Popular Education', in R. Hooper (ed.), *The Curriculum: Context, Design and Development* (Edinburgh, Oliver and Boyd, 1971) is a frankly elitist argument for separate curricula, for the working class, on the one hand, and the middle and upper classes, on the other. As a corrective, look at Gingell and Brandon, *In Defence of High Culture* (Oxford, Blackwell, 2000). One of the earliest works to advocate something like a national curriculum was John White's *Towards a Compulsory Curriculum* (London, Routledge, 1973). Paul Hirst's *Knowledge and the Curriculum* (London, Routledge, 1974) sets out an epistemological justification for a full liberal curriculum. John White's *The Aims of Education Restated* (London, Routledge, 1982) and Christopher Winch's *Quality and Education* (Oxford, Blackwell, 1996) both contain discussions of the relationship between the aims of education and the curriculum. Steven Bramall and John White's *Will the New National Curriculum Live up to its Aims?* (London, Philosophy of Education Society of Great Britain, 2000) assesses the validity of the 1999 aims for the English school curriculum. On specific curricular issues, Kevin Williams' *Why Teach Foreign Languages in Schools?* (London, Philosophy of Education Society of Great Britain, 2000) questions the role of modern foreign languages as a compulsory curriculum element.

Chapter 3

Teaching and learning
Knowledge and the imagination

This chapter begins by looking at the nature of teaching and considers the relationship between teaching and learning. It is argued that, although one cannot expect learning always to be the result of teaching, teachers do have to show that they have not been negligent in regard of pupils' learning. Successful learning involves, in some sense, 'getting it right' or conforming to standards of what counts as knowledge in a particular subject matter. This does not mean that there has to be a comprehensive theory of learning. Indeed, it is doubtful whether any such thing exists. It is also important to appreciate that learning also involves becoming able to do certain things as well as acquiring factual information. Education needs to keep the practical and non-practical aspects of learning in balance, not place undue emphasis on either one or the other. Education is also concerned with developing the imagination, but this is best achieved, not through the promotion of a doubtful faculty of creativity, but by allowing pupils to see the imagination at work in the achievements of individuals in a wide range of worthwhile endeavours.

The nature of teaching

Teaching and learning are at the heart of the educational enterprise and, therefore, are the activities we would expect to characterise our educational institutions. Given that this is the case, we might also expect that philosophers of education would have used their time and expertise to clarify these important concepts. While such an expectation is, largely, satisfied with regard to teaching, it is far from clear that this is the case with learning. The asymmetry is even more surprising given that most analyses of 'teaching' assume an intimate connection – logical or otherwise – between it and 'learning'.

Let us begin to spell out the situation with some minimally controversial points. All the commentators upon teaching seem to agree that there can be no simple behavioural definition of the term (see Hirst 1973; Scheffler 1973). What this means is that, given an appropriate context, a vast range of behaviours, including such things as standing on one's head, looking out of the window, pointing at the wall, might count as part of teaching. Teaching is centrally, if not entirely (see below), a purposeful activity and there may be a myriad of behaviours which help – or hinder – its purposes.

The second point which is widely – if not universally – accepted is that teaching involves a triadic relationship between a teacher, something that is taught and someone who is taught. We sometimes conceal one of the necessary elements that composes teaching when we, loosely, describe someone as simply 'teaching mathematics' or 'teaching 3C'. But it only takes a moment's reflection to see that one cannot be doing the first unless one is teaching mathematics *to someone*, i.e. it would make no sense to talk of teaching mathematics in an empty classroom, and one can only teach 3C if one is teaching them *something*. In the recent past, one of the slogans of the progressive or child-centred educational was that 'we teach children not subjects'. If such a slogan was simply meant to remind us that there is always someone to be taught as well as something we are teaching, then it might function as a useful reminder. If, however, it was meant to imply that we can teach without teaching some content, then the slogan is incoherent.

Given this triadic relationship between a teacher, a subject matter and a learner, how close is the relationship between the three things? If someone is teaching something to someone, *must* this mean that the someone is learning what is taught? If someone is learning, must there be a teacher who is teaching them? On these questions philosophers of education disagree about the answers. In America there were attempts to explicate an analogy initially suggested by John Dewey (1933) between teaching and learning and buying and selling. If such an analogy is correct, then there would be a logical relationship between the two terms. Just as it is impossible to sell something without a buyer, or to buy something without a seller, then it would be impossible to teach without somebody learning or to learn without somebody teaching. But this is surely mistaken. It is, after all, commonplace for people to learn things, e.g. that fire burns, that there are three green doors in the street, without a teacher. And most teachers would not withdraw the claim that they had been teaching on being told that not everyone in their class had learned everything that they had been taught.

A better account of teaching, perhaps, focuses not directly upon the outcome of learning but rather upon learning as an intended outcome. So, teaching is an activity intended to bring about learning (see Hirst and Peters 1970; Scheffler 1973). But such a criterion on its own is not sufficient to guarantee teaching. It would not, for instance, distinguish between someone trying to teach but failing to do so and someone actually teaching. Given this gap, there have been various suggestions for filling it. Hirst and Peters suggested the addition of an indicative criterion, that the intended teacher must be doing things with the subject matter, e.g. lecturing on it, demonstrating it, illustrating it, which indicates their purposes to the learner. They also suggested a 'readiness' condition, that learners must be ready, in terms of age and capability, to learn the intended subject matter. Scheffler combines these two in the notion that the teacher must be engaged in activities which are likely to bring about the learning which is intended. But he added that what the teacher does must fall under certain restrictions of manner, e.g. so that torture or brainwashing are not allowed.

There are technical difficulties with such analyses which show another aspect of teaching. These difficulties concern the weight of the supporting conditions. Let us suppose, for instance, that someone is doing everything we think that can be done – apart from torture, brainwashing, etc. – to bring about learning. Given that this is the case, then it is likely that learning will occur. But, if the satisfaction of the supporting conditions make this so, then why do we need the initial condition concerned with intention?

We call this a 'technical' difficulty because, as a matter of fact, we would not expect the supporting conditions to be fulfilled unless the initial condition was also satisfied. And, as a matter of policy, we want teachers in our educational institutions who both intend that people learn and do all that is possible to ensure that such learning takes place. But the difficulty does seem to indicate that unintentional teaching could take place. This may be important for various aspects of education which are often neglected. So, for example, it is at least arguable that moral education proceeds by exemplification rather than – or as well as – instruction. Children learn to be honest, kind, fair, etc. by those around them exemplifying such virtues. But such exemplification seems to preclude the possibility that the dominant intention here is one concerned with passing on the virtue in question. If you only act in a kindly manner because you wish another to imitate you, then the lesson you are really teaching is about insincerity rather than kindness. We can also apply this insight to the normal teaching of subjects within education. One of the things that any good teacher hopes is that their pupils learn to care about such subjects. Such caring again precludes the possibility that the primary motive here has to do with the pupil rather than the teacher's relationship to his or her subject. If the teacher is concentrating upon the pupils noticing and being influenced by their care for the subject, they seem to have lost the appropriate focus of such care, which is for the subject itself.

We may couch the above in terms of responsibility. Teachers are responsible for their pupils learning and such responsibility goes beyond the holding of a set of appropriate intentions. Teachers may well be responsible if their pupils learn things from them, e.g. that it is justifiable to be bad-tempered on Monday morning, even though such learning was no part of their intention. But this does not mean, as some have held (see Kleinig 1982), that teachers have a total responsibility for their pupils learning. It does not mean that if pupils do not learn, then the teacher must have been negligent in some way. Negligence involves the bringing about of harm avoidably but unintentionally. In this case the harm is someone failing to learn. Such a failure *might* indicate negligence. However, the defence against negligence is not merely that the harm did not occur but also that it was unavoidable. Thus, if a teacher can show that they have done everything possible to avoid the outcome, then they have shown that they are not at fault. However, if we take teachers' responsibility seriously and if we have cases where pupils consistently fail to learn – or learn inappropriate things – then such a situation should lead us to ask for such a demonstration of lack of fault.

Learning

What about the *learning* involved in teaching and learning? As we mentioned at the beginning of this chapter, philosophers have been strangely silent upon this topic. An analysis of the concept of 'learning' seems a relatively straightforward affair. The standard case of learning involves an individual acquiring knowledge that they did not have before. Such knowledge may be a question of familiarisation, e.g. I know what X looks like; or propositional knowledge, e.g. I now know the truth of some proposition, such as the Battle of Hastings took place in 1066; or a piece of procedural knowledge, i.e. a piece of know how, e.g. how to ride a bike. Because knowledge, in all its forms, implies an idea of correctness, i.e. getting something right, the standard case also involves such correctness. So, for instance, if some claim that they have become familiar with the look of Joe Bloggs, then we expect them to be able to recognise Joe Bloggs. If they claim to have learned the date of the Battle of Hastings, we assume both that the battle did take place in 1066 and that they will respond in the appropriate way when, for instance, they are asked the date of the battle. If someone claims to have learned how to ride a bike, then we expect them to be able to ride a bike. Of course, in all these cases someone may have learned something without giving us evidence that this is so, e.g. they may refuse to acknowledge that it is Joe Bloggs, or refuse to answer a question about the battle, or refuse to get on the bike. However, such cases must be substandard in some way. Unless we could reliably check whether someone had learned something most of the time – and this applies to our own learning as well as the learning of others – then our notions of what it is to learn would have no solid grip on reality.

There are other substandard cases of learning. Just as we may be informed about something, e.g. the look of Joe Bloggs or the date of the battle, we may also be misinformed. We may think we know, although we, in fact, do not. And the same applies to procedural knowledge; we may think we know how to do something without being able to do it.

While the standard case above implies the successful achievement of learning, educators are also interested in the processes of coming to learn. Thus, if I have learned the details of William the Conqueror's campaign for the conquest of England I will know the date of the Battle of Hastings. If, on the other hand, I am learning about the campaign, then, although it is likely that I will know some of the relevant facts, there is no particular fact that I have to know to sustain the claim that I am learning. Here, as elsewhere, the standard case provides the guidelines. If we did not know what the achievement of learning looked like, we would have no way of identifying the processes of learning. So we could not say that pupils were engaged in learning activities if we had no idea of what it would mean for them to have learned something successfully.

It is probably the case that learning is a primitive concept. That is that we may explain the lives of human beings – and some other animals – in terms of their capacity to learn but we may not be able to explain this capacity. Any attempt to do so is likely to simply assume that which it is supposed to explain. Thus, for example, one of the modern imperatives that educators are supposed to obey is to encourage their pupils 'to learn how to learn' (this probably originates in the Deschooling Movement, see Barrow 1978, Chapter 7). But such a notion simply assumes that such pupils can learn how to learn how to learn. Without this initial assumption of an underlying capacity to learn, the imperative would make no sense.

It may be the case that the recognition by philosophers of education that learning is a primitive concept had led to their relative silence on the subject. After all, if it is primitive in the given sense, then there is very little to say. However, this has not prevented others from trying to establish theories of learning. Typically, in the twentieth century, such theories have clustered around psychological theories such as behaviourism and cognitivism. If such theories are credible, then it may be the case that they could generate approaches to teaching which would help to facilitate successful learning. However, there seem to be very good reasons for supposing that such approaches are not credible (see Winch 1998) and it is certainly the case that no such theory has, as yet, generated such approaches to teaching. Rather, we get the promotion of half-baked ideas, such as that we should aim at 'active' learning which either ignores the fact that all learning, by its very nature must be active, i.e. must involve mental change, or, in designating certain activities, e.g. sitting listening in a lecture, reading a book, as passive, ignores the fact that much learning does go on in such circumstances. (The irony here is that such proponents of 'active' learning spread the word through lectures and books.)

Learning may be primitive but it is not conditionless. All the standard examples of learning that we have given – and by implication the teaching that might bring about such learning – involve the learner getting better at something. So, in all cases, the learner moves from ignorance to knowledge. And, in theory at least, we can know that such progress has taken place. Learning by its very nature is progressive. Where such progress is impossible, then learning cannot take place.

The last sentence might be taken as an empty truism except for the fact that in large parts of education it seems to be ignored. So, for example, it seems to us, based upon our experience of teaching philosophy courses concerned with values, e.g. Moral Philosophy and Aesthetics, that a large proportion of pupils leave school, after having studied subjects such as art and literature, convinced that the values involved in such subjects are subjective. Crudely, that to say that an X is good – where X is a work of art or an action – is simply to say that you like X. To say that X is better than Y is another way of saying that you prefer X to Y.

Now it may be the case that such subjectivism is, in fact, true; that there are no objective values either in art or elsewhere (but see Gingell and Brandon 2000, Chapter 3). But if this is true, then this means that no learning is possible in those areas in which it is true. If all values are simply preferences and if all preferences are as good as one another, i.e. there is no objective standard which can be applied to such preferences, then it becomes impossible to learn to be a *better* valuer. And this means that all of these activities, from wine tasting to a degree in Art History or English Literature, which seem to assume that such progress is possible, are simply a waste of time. Of course, it may be the case that, by taking part in such activities one's preferences change, but, because one set of preferences, on this theory, cannot be better than any other set, then such a change hardly seems to merit the label of improvement and therefore justify the hard work involved.

The position can be couched in terms of expertise. Teaching and learning involve the teacher passing on, or trying to pass on, their expertise to the learner. Subjectivism claims that, as far as values are concerned, no one can be more expert than anyone else, i.e. if everyone is equally an expert, the notion of expertise becomes completely redundant, but if this is so, then it becomes impossible to either pass on expertise or endeavour to become more expert.

The varieties of knowledge

We have already touched upon the types of knowledge we would expect to be developed by pupils within education. These are knowledge by acquaintance, propositional knowledge, i.e. knowledge that some proposition is true or false, and procedural knowledge, i.e. know-how. Although there are overlaps between the three types, it is probably the case that none of the types can be completely reduced to the others. There have been attempts, most notably by Paul Hirst in the 1960s and 1970s (see Hirst 1974, for a collection of papers connected with this issue) to establish one of the types of knowledge as of paramount import-ance for education. Hirst argued that, if we think of education as the develop-ment of the rational mind and then ask for the content of such a mind, we shall come to see such content as being made up of the different forms of knowledge which have been developed over the centuries. Each form of knowledge, Hirst claimed, would embody central concepts which are particular to that form, e.g. gravity and acceleration in science, God and sin in religion, good and wrong in moral knowledge. Each will display a distinctive logical structure which will determine what can and cannot be said within the form. And, most import-antly, each will throw up expressions which are testable against experience for their truth. It is this last condition which shows that this is a theory concerning propositional knowledge. According to Hirst, in the paper which introduced this theory (Hirst 1965a), there are essentially eight forms of propositional knowledge: mathematics, physical sciences, human sciences, history, religion, literature and the fine arts, philosophy, morality. While Hirst never claimed that only the eight forms should be studied at school – he left room for other non-academic concerns – and also never claimed that each had to be approached in its pure form – the individual forms could be combined and studied in 'fields of knowledge', e.g. geography with its roots in the physical and human sciences is such a field – it is nevertheless true that Hirst's theory seemed to offer a clear and neat basis for the academic curriculum. But only, of course, if the theory was sound. Confidence in the soundness of the theory was rather undermined by the fact that Hirst himself seemed to have difficulty deciding what was and was not a form of knowledge. So, in 1965, he published a paper (Hirst 1965b) arguing that religion was not, and could not be, a form of knowledge. In later articulation of the theory the human sciences and history were merged to become 'knowledge of oneself and other people' and part of philosophy was moved to mathematics so that this became 'logic and mathematics'. But it was also the case that the theory was the subject of concerted criticism (see, for instance, Barrow 1976; Gingell 1985) which sought to show that the epistemological basis of the theory was misconceived and that certain of the putative forms of knowledge, e.g. religion, morality and especially literature and the fine arts, were only pretenders to knowledge. Hirst never replied directly to such attacks but in the 1990s (see Hirst 1993) he repudiated the theory because, he claimed, it gave too little attention to know-how and cultural transmission.

While Hirst's theory, with its emphasis upon propositional knowledge, was moving from the centre stage, another theory with a totally different emphasis threatened to take its place. This was an account of knowledge based on a distinction originally argued for in Gilbert Ryle's classic *The Concept of Mind* (1949). Ryle, in that work, while acknowledging the role of propositional knowledge in the human mind, argues that at least as great a role is played by procedural knowledge, i.e. know-how, which cannot be reduced to knowledge of propositions. Thus, our knowledge of how to ride a bike, or how to swim, is essentially practical and, because of this, it can only be tested in practice. It certainly cannot be tested by uttering any list of true propositions concerning cycling or swimming. The seeming strength of Hirst's theory was the close connection apparently established between knowledge, truth and rationality. The strength of Ryle's theory seems to be the connection that can be established between know-how and intelligence. Thus, Ryle argued (see Ryle 1974), that it is not knowledge of facts, i.e. propositional knowledge, which shows intelligence, but rather, knowing how to organise such facts that you do command, so, for instance, someone with few facts at their fingertips may deal with these much more intelligently than someone who knows many such facts. The appeal of such a theory for education should be obvious. Not only does its emphasis on the practical open up educational possibilities beyond the realm of knowledge of truth, then why shouldn't the former have as much a place in education as the latter? But it also seems to show where our emphasis within subjects should lie. Just as with mathematics, we are concerned that children learn how to do maths, rather than simply learn a set of mathematical truths, e.g. the tables, then, with this theory in front of us, surely children should also learn how to do history or science rather than just learning historical and scientific facts (it is at least arguable that there is at least some emphasis on these kinds of procedures in Hirst as well).

This type of change of emphasis has been a welcome feature of English education in the past twenty years although it entered under a rather misleading banner (see below). However, the emphasis needs to be handled with caution. First, there is a danger of children wasting a vast amount of time in any subject by doing the equivalent of reinventing the wheel. While, of course, we want children to know how to do maths or history, the basic facts in such subjects, e.g. the times tables or a respectable chronology of events, are not an impediment to such know-how, but rather, a good practical aid. Second, and Ryle's arguments notwithstanding, while we can begin to teach our pupils how to ask the right questions about, say, a poem or historical primary sources, they probably cannot get satisfactory answers to such questions without a background of factual knowledge. So, for instance, one might provide history students with source material concerning industrialisation in nineteenth-century Lancashire and although they can begin to engage critically with the documents, they probably cannot reach a reasonable assessment of such material without a knowledge of the process of industrialisation elsewhere in the country. Third, while it is pleasant seeing literature students providing their own analyses of, say, poems rather than simply parroting the judgements of the established critics, there is no doubt that very often our own ideas are reached through thinking about the views of others. And it is certainly the case that one cannot appreciate the genius of Shakespeare or Wordsworth without knowing about the work of their predecessors or contemporaries.

What the above shows is that while practical or procedural knowledge may be one of the proper focuses of education, it is something to be aimed at in balance with the other types of knowledge. Propositional knowledge often provides the context in which such knowledge can develop and flourish, and knowledge by acquaintance can be seen as providing the objects, e.g. poems or pieces of historical source material, which enable the other types of knowledge to grow.

There is another danger with an exclusive focus upon procedural knowledge. Although, as we said above, emphasis upon it provides a welcome chance to widen the curriculum, taken alone, it threatens to make it both too wide and also too shallow. There is an enormous range of such knowledge; everything from knowing how to make a bed to knowing how to do philosophy or nuclear physics, and unless we have some way of deciding which of it to include within formal education, we are threatened with a curriculum that is huge, amorphous and, often, trivial. Thus, such an emphasis also needs to be coupled with the type of cultural constraints we mentioned in our chapter on the curriculum. In this way we can ensure that children begin to know how to engage in certain activities but, at the same time, ensure that the activities chosen are worth their engagement.

We said above that procedural knowledge entered the educational arena under a misleading banner. Although concern about the development of such knowledge derives from the work of Ryle, such concern, which has been apparent in educational circles at all levels for the past twenty years, often is introduced under the label of 'skill'. So, for instance, primary school teachers are often told to pay attention to their pupils' reading and writing skills and their speaking and listening skills, and university departments are charged to attend to the subject-specific and transferable skills they expect their students to develop. While part of what Ryle was saying can be made to fit, fairly comfortably, with this notion of skill, part of it cannot. And it is striking that Ryle himself does nothing to encourage the identification of procedural knowledge and skill. The reason for this may be that there is only a partial overlap between the two concepts. There is disagreement about the meaning of 'skill' talk (Barrow 1987; Smith 1987). However, it seems likely that any reasonable use of the concept of 'skill' has to be based in some way upon the notion of skilful performance of some task or other. But, if this is so, then much skill talk becomes misleading. It is certainly the case that some of the things that people can be taught how to do can be done, more or less, skilfully. So, someone may be taught how to analyse a poem or ride a bike and their performances can properly be judged in terms of its skilfulness. At the bottom end of this continuum will be mere workmanlike performances while at the top end such performances will approximate to the expert practitioners such as F.R. Leavis or Lance Armstrong. But, even in such cases, the teacher's concern may not be with the possible heights that can be reached. The bike riding instructor may judge himself completely successful if his pupil can stay on the bike and negotiate a public road in traffic without expecting, or even hoping, that such a pupil would go on to win the Tour de France. However, with some of the things that are collected under talk of skills, such variation of performance is difficult to imagine. So, for instance, some people talk of 'library skills' where what they seem to mean is being able to find a book in a library. It really is very difficult to see how such book finding could be done, more or less, skilfully. The awarding of a prize for a student's philosophy essay seems perfectly understandable but the notion of such a prize for 'library skills' seems ludicrous. The same is true with something like 'listening skills'. In the normal, general context people listen to what is being said to them or do not. They do not, because they cannot listen more or less skilfully. This is not to say that people may not be taught how to listen or how to use a library catalogue, only that such lessons, because they can have little to do with skilful performance, are dubiously to do with skills.

This issue can be dealt with by noting the difference between mere competence and skill and by seeing that, very often, it is the first of these that we are aiming at in our teaching and, in many cases, this is all that can be sensibly aimed at. But this distinction does not help us at all with some skills talk. When people start talking 'caring' skills or 'friendship' skills or 'religious' skills, it is very difficult to see what they mean at all. Neither notions of competence nor notions of skilfulness seem to have any purchase in such talk. But if this is so, then it is likely that what is going on is another, and completely redundant, way of talking about caring, being friendly and being religious. And because it is redundant we have no need of such talk, it obscures rather than reveals the topic in hand.

The importance of imagination

We want the people being taught in our educational institutions to come to know things in all the senses of knowledge. But we want more than this. Simply to emphasise knowledge in this way would be to see education as solely concerned with cultural reproduction in a completely static sense, i.e. such knowledge would merely reproduce what we already know. There is no doubt that some educational systems have only been concerned with this. Thus, a primitive tribe or a peasant society in a stable world may wish that their children come to know the things which will enable them to replace their parents and nothing more. (Anything more might be looked upon either as dangerously radical or a waste of time.) But such stasis cannot be *our* aim, partly, because we are aware that the world is rapidly changing and we want our children to be able to cope with such changes. And partly, because in wanting a liberal educational system we are committed to trying to produce people who can exercise autonomous choice and such choice implies that possibility of going beyond what is already known. The successful students in such a liberal system will not merely imbibe the received wisdom of our culture but will critically engage with it. They are learning not merely what we consider valuable but how to create value for themselves, to become the producers of the culture of tomorrow, as well as the receivers of the culture of yesterday. But to do this they need more than just knowledge, they need imagination.

Very few people would, we hope, deny the claim that education should develop the imagination of these being educated. And yet such a claim is fraught with difficulty. We simply do not have a fully worked out theory of the imagination and the history of philosophy seems to offer few real clues. So, for instance, the great eighteenth-century Scottish philosopher David Hume, at times, sees the imagination as the source of dangerous, fanciful notions, but at other times, sees it as productive of the only coherent picture of the world that we might have. The writer Charles Dickens, who devoted his novel *Hard Times* to a defence of the imagination, seemed to see it as merely the faculty for producing entertaining fancies. Both writers under-estimate the scope and importance of the imagination but we have, as yet, no fully articulated theory to challenge their partial visions. The elements of such a theory are being developed in the work of philosophers such as Kendall Walton (see Walton 1990) but Walton would certainly not claim either to have covered all such elements or to have fully investigated these elements which he does deal with. Walton's analysis begins with, but goes far beyond, the notion of the imagination as the way in which we entertain propositions or suppose that certain states of affairs might obtain. Such a basic notion sees the use of the imagination as the way in which we envisage possibilities. And such a notion, although it is basic, gives us some idea of the importance of the imagination. Without it no works of art could be produced; for artists are involved in making what they consider as possible into something that is actual. But it goes far beyond art. All values, because they go beyond the mere facts of the case, also involve the envisaging of possibilities. All progress in any human endeavour, or, at least, all deliberate attempts to initiate such progress, also involves the consideration of possibilities. Whether we are talking about physics, politics, philosophy or cookery, no such progress can come about without someone wondering, about possibilities that do not yet exist, that is, someone saying to themselves, 'What if . . . ?' or 'Suppose that . . .'. If this is correct, then the imagination and its cultivation must be central concerns for any programme of liberal education. However, to make a case for the development of the imagination within such a programme is to do nothing to show how it is to be developed. We will return to this problem after a short digression.

Most of the discussion concerning the development of the imagination among English educationalists comes as a subtext of another discussion. This concerns the development of 'creativity' among children in our schools. There was good work done by philosophers in the 1970s (see White 1968; Woods and Barrow 1975) which could be seen as a warning against such a focus for education. However, although some of the lessons of such writers have been learned, their general caution about the development of creativity has gone, largely, unheeded. So, in 1999, the National Advisory Committee on Creative and Cultural Education published its report *All Our Futures: Creativity, Culture and Education* which was the result of consultation with over two hundred significant figures within the arts and education. While the report does not offer the depth or argument which we get in the philosophical texts, its definition of 'creativity' has striking similarities to the previous work. So, for the authors of the report, creative processes must possess four characteristics:

> Firstly, they always involve thinking or behaving imaginatively. Second, overall this imaginative activity is purposeful; that is, it is directed to achieving an objective. Third, these processes must generate something original. Fourth, the outcome must be of value in relation to the objective. We therefore define creativity as: imaginative activity fashioned so as to produce outcomes that are both original and of value.
>
> (ibid., p. 29)

The philosophical work mentioned above typically uses a paradigm case argument to establish its definition of creativity. In such an argument you take examples of people – or work – which are, fairly uncontroversially, creative and then generalise from such examples. So we look at the works of figures such as Beethoven, Shakespeare, Einstein, Picasso, Tolstoy, etc., then distil the features that such work had in common. While the report does not overtly use this approach, its use of quotations from figures such as Einstein, Henry Ford, Martha Graham and various Nobel-winning scientists, suggests that such an approach is hovering in the background. We are convinced that the paradigm case analysis is the way to achieve a reasonable definition of 'creativity'. However, we are also convinced that, in achieving this, all the writers concerned simply come to rob the term of any real educational significance.

We can see this by the definitions offered in the Report of 'originality'. According to the authors of the Report:

> Creativity always involves originality. But there are different categories of originality.
>
> Individual
> A person's work may be original in relation to their own previous work and output.
>
> Relative
> It may be original in relation to their peer groups: to other young people of the same age.
>
> Historic
> The work may be original in terms of anyone's previous output in a particular field: that is it may be uniquely original.
>
> (ibid., p. 30)

The third category here sits easily with the paradigm case argument. We are here talking of the production of a *Hamlet*, *The School of Athens*, *The Emperor Concerto* or *War and Peace*: works which significantly alter their particular fields. But the first two categories are *nothing like this at all*! If we take 'original' to mean, with the authors of the report, new and valuable, and then apply this to the other categories, we can see the yawning chasm between these and the third.

So, for instance, children – and students generally – throughout their education are learning new things and such new things will, hopefully, be of value to them. So this type of individual originality will be a typical feature of education. The 'relative' category fares little better. Of course, some children will outstrip their year groups and, often, such outstripping will have a perfectly straightforward explanation, e.g. they may come from academically well endowed and supportive backgrounds. But, again, this is hardly out of the ordinary. But the whole point of the third category, i.e. historic originality, is that it refers to the truly extraordinary. Not to the work of the slightly above average writer, painter, composer or what have you, but to the productions of the greatest – and because of the way such definitions work, unquestionably greatest – practitioners in their field. Not to people who get better as they go along, or slightly outstrip their fellow workers; but to people who change everything in their respective fields.

The mistake being made by the writers of the report, and it is a very important mistake both for our discussion and educational generally, is to confuse two distinct categories of achievement. On the one hand, we have very broad categories like intelligence or imagination which we can relativise to apply to the work of 5-year-olds and, on the other, to the work of the masters in their fields. So, for instance, it makes perfect sense to praise a school child for producing work that is more imaginative than she has ever produced before or is more imaginative than that of her peers. With the historic category we are *not* talking about such a broad continuum. We are talking about work of genius and, while it may make sense to see this as covering a small group of people, e.g. Marlowe as well as Shakespeare, Dickens and well as Tolstoy, it would be dangerous hyperbole to apply this to children in school. Even if we look at the juvenilia of people such as Wordsworth or Picasso, we see works of great promise but nothing which yet deserves the accolade of genius.

Does this mistake matter? Surely all that is going on here is that the authors of the report are displaying an over-enthusiastic, but generally beneficent, ambition for our children? We think that the mistake does matter for several reasons. First, in endorsing the aim and objectives for children in our schools – and for those teaching them – which they cannot possibly achieve, the authors of the report threaten to waste a great deal of precious educational time. In attempting to gerrymander the boundaries of creativity to include the typical achievements of some people – or atypical but not surprising achievement of others – the report may blind people to the real and outstanding achievements of others and, at the same time, divert them away from the type of thing which might provide realistic, but commendable, aspirations for their own work. If you persuade people, for instance, that their first faltering rhymes are on a par with Shakespeare, you distort their own achievements and capabilities – which may be real – and block any real appreciation of Shakespeare and obscure the possibility of such appreciation.

Second, if we assume, as do the authors of the report and almost all other writers on 'creativity' that this is a proper focus of educational concern, this will tend to prevent a proper and critical look at what happens and might happen within our systems of education. The result of such a realistic survey might show something like the following: Arts education in our schools is deeply unsatisfactory. It is not merely that it does not, because it cannot, produce creative pupils in the proper sense of the term, but that, in areas such as painting and music, most pupils end up, after a period of eleven years of compulsory schooling where countless hours are spent on such things, as artistic illiterates. The contrast with the teaching of literature is telling here. For the most part such teaching has never had, as its primary aim, the production of creative writers. Rather the aim has been the cultivation of appreciation. And, while this aim has never been completely realised, we have, nevertheless, ended up with a culture where a vast number of people prize and enjoy literature. And this, in turn, may encourage those who wish to write. The teachers of literature have manifested a realistic expectation of what schools can do. They are places where pupils do, or should, learn about the achievements of Shakespeare, Wordsworth or Milton. They are not places where we can produce a Shakespeare, a Wordsworth or a Milton for this we do not know how to do!

If we couch what has just been said in terms of the cultivation of the imagination, and widen our curricular concerns, this conclusion seems to follow. The best way we know of developing the imagination of people being taught is to get them to appreciate the imagination of others. Such imagination can be seen within the work of the great artists we have mentioned, but it can also be seen in the scientific work of a Newton or an Einstein, or the mathematical work of Euclid or Riemann. Once we see that areas such as science and mathematics are fields in which the imagination has an important place we begin to understand the excitement and cultural importance of such areas. And just as a proper education in art and music would do much to remedy the dire situation that we have today, a proper education in mathematics and the sciences would begin to produce people who would understand how scientists such as Newton and Darwin changed everything and why the work of Euclid served as an intellectual model for two thousand years.

In terms of the topics of this chapter: teaching and learning and what, in general, is to be learned, the faults of our education systems in the past have largely to be located in a lack of ambition for children as such or for particular types of children, e.g. working-class children or girls. So certain things were thought to be either beyond the capabilities of all or some children or to be completely unnecessary for their education. Such attitudes did a great deal of educational damage. However, just as damaging is to have completely unrealistic expectations of what children might achieve at any stage of their education. If we ignore logic and common sense and try to do what cannot be done, this must be at the expense of trying to achieve worthwhile but realistic goals. We may not, because we cannot, teach every child to be an Einstein or a Wordsworth, but this does not mean that we cannot, given time and appropriate effort, produce children who can understand and appreciate what the Einsteins and Wordsworths of the past have contributed to our knowledge and understanding. And if this is the most that we can do, it is surely far from a worthless goal.

Conclusion

The notions of teaching and learning, knowledge and imagination, are fundamental to our understanding and expectations with regard to education. If we do not have full, but realistic, conceptions of what the scope and limits of such concepts are, we cannot begin to grasp what might be attempted within our schools. All these notions are complicated and with imagination we are only at the beginning of a satisfactory analysis of the complications. The enemies to clarity here are either a too simple view of the concept in question, e.g. so that one type of knowledge becomes *the* aim of teaching, or a too ambitious view of what can be done within education, e.g. so that we expect children to produce work on a par with that of a genius. It is certainly the case that in the past we have lacked ambition when it comes to the achievement of children within our schools. However, this is to be remedied by realistic aspirations and not by wishing for the impossible.

Questions for further discussion

1   What should you say to someone who says 'I teach children, not subjects'? Would it differ from what you would say to someone who says 'I teach subjects, not children'?
2   Could someone be teaching if no-one in their class learned anything?
3   Why do many educators dislike rote learning? Do you think that they are wrong to disapprove of it in all circumstances?
4   How should a subjectivist teach art?
5   Is the teaching of creative writing to primary schoolchildren based on a philosophical mistake about creativity?

Further reading

The classic readings on the relationship between teaching and learning are to be found in R.S. Peters (ed.), *The Philosophy of Education* (Oxford, Oxford University Press, 1966), see also John Kleinig, *Philosophical Issues in Education* (London, Croom Helm, 1982), Chapters 3 and 4.

For detailed discussion of the nature of learning, see David Hamlyn, *Experience and the Growth of Understanding* (London, Routledge, 1978), and Christopher Winch, *The Philosophy of Human Learning* (London, Routledge, 1998). For a more summary treatment, see David Carr, *Making Sense of Education* (London, Routledge, 2003), Chapter 6.

A defence of the role of creativity in education is to be found in H. Lytton, *Creativity and Education* (London, Routledge, 1971). For a more modest defence of its role, see David Best, *The Rationality of Feeling* (Brighton, Falmer, 1992), Chapter 7. The claim is, however, subject to sustained criticism by Ronald Woods and Robin Barrow, *Introduction to the Philosophy of Education* (London, Methuen, 1975), Chapter 8, and John Gingell, 'Against Creativity', *Irish Educational Studies*, vol. 20, pp. 25–37 (2001).

Chapter 4

Pedagogy, good practice and educational research

This chapter continues the topic of the previous one in pursuing the question of what counts as *good* teaching. We begin by considering some of the pitfalls that those who broach this subject may encounter. We then go on to consider the vexed issue of what counts as 'good practice' in teaching and uncover a conceptual minefield. The chapter then moves on to a critical discussion of those philosophers of education who hold views that suggest that there is no evidence from research that can be brought to bear on the question as to whether or not teaching can be improved. We show that, ultimately, these arguments contain insurmountable logical flaws. We conclude by setting out the case for evidence-based pedagogy.

What is pedagogy?

It is fairly unusual to have a chapter concerned with pedagogy, i.e. the science of teaching, in a book concerned with the philosophy of education. Partly, this is because philosophers have been generally sceptical about the evidence of such a science; and partly because even those philosophers who might think that there are things to be known about effective teaching see the matter as a case for empirical research or common sense rather than philosophical reflection. We have some sympathy with both these attitudes. We suspect that any attempt to produce recipes for teaching which aspire to scientific rigour must fail. We also believe that, by and large, it is factual research rather than philosophical argument which should underpin effective teaching. However, we also think that there are interesting philosophical issues here concerned with the conceptualisation of good practice within teaching, the ways in which notions of good practice involve a careful consideration of educational aims and the very possibility of establishing relevant factual research. In this chapter we will explore these issues.

First, however, it is useful to explain what we mean by 'pedagogy'. In the previous chapter we explained at length what we understood the term 'teaching' to mean. We concluded that teaching was an intentional activity for which the teacher had primary responsibility. However, teachers could not *guarantee* that their pupils learned what they intended them to learn. We *can* however, expect teachers to take all reasonable steps to ensure that pupils learn what it is intended by their teachers that they should learn. A teacher's *pedagogy*, then, is the method or methods which he or she employs in getting children to learn. It may include training, instruction, explanation, demonstration, assessment and setting up structured opportunities for pupils to learn. It may include one or more of these elements in various combinations according to the teaching task and the classroom context. Whatever it is, the teacher is responsible for ensuring that the right mix of methods is used.

How, then, does the teacher decide what technique or combination of techniques he or she should use? The answer is implicit in the account of teaching that we have offered. The teacher needs to employ those techniques that are considered most likely to produce the results that he or she is aiming for in their pupils' learning. There is no *a priori* answer to this question: that is, one that rests on deduction from first principles. Those, like Rousseau ([1762] 1910) who have thought so, have assumed that there are very general principles of psychology that apply to all humans at all times and must be followed if teaching is not to lead to failure or even disaster. Many educators have rightly become suspicious of pedagogy based on such sweeping generalisations. However, they have sometimes been led into two opposite errors, of assuming *either* that there is no evidence relevant to the question of whether pedagogy is effective or not, *or* that it is impossible to make any general points about what is pedagogically effective. We reject all three of these views and argue for pedagogical practice that is not only based on the teacher's intentions, but also on what the empirical evidence suggests is the most effective way of achieving those intentions.

Before we can move on to a defence of this view, we need to clear one issue out of the way, which is bound up with the very common use of the phrase 'good practice'. There are senses of the use of this term which have nothing to do with evidence, but with strongly held moral beliefs about what it is acceptable to do with children. These again are often based on the kind of general psychological theory of someone like Rousseau or his followers, or of a more scientifically minded educational thinker like Jean Piaget or Noam Chomsky. Our view of this is that all teaching must conform to the ethical standards that apply in the community and to what the teacher can, in all conscience, sanction as a teaching method. Thus, brainwashing, cruelty, intimidation, manipulation and deception are to be excluded from any pedagogical practice. However, this leaves a great deal to play for. We argue that what is left to play for is largely dependent on evidence as to what is or is not effective in achieving given aims. Our first task is to 'deconstruct' the problematic notion of good practice.

Good practice and its problems

It would seem to be the case that the search for an effective teaching method is essentially the search for what constitutes good practice in the classroom. Thus, a teacher of, say, History, might wonder whether a whole class approach, involving copious note taking and general discussion, is the best way of proceeding or whether it might be better to join the children into small groups, give them some source material and let them discuss such material among themselves. With this latter approach the teacher acts as an advisor to the individual groups and, perhaps, brings the class together to discuss the conclusions of the groups at the end of the process. This appears to be the type of problem concerning method that teachers might, realistically, find themselves in. If it is, however, the teacher in question will get very little guidance from much of the literature concerning good practice in education. So, for instance, a report by Her Majesty's Inspectorate (HMI) on one teacher training institution in the UK found that:

> The college declares publicly its philosophy of good primary practice ... This philosophy has several key elements. These are stated to include:
>
> • The recognition of the uniqueness of the individual child.
> • The importance of first-hand experience.
> • The value of an attractive and stimulating learning environment.
>
> (H.M.S.O. 1991, *Bishop Grosseteste College: A Report by H.M.I.*, cited in Alexander 1992, p. 181)

Such an account of good practice offers nothing to our teacher with a problem. It makes no mention of the content of education and therefore completely bypasses his or her concern to teach History. But it also avoids any substantive concern with methodology so that it gives no real advice on how to teach. And therefore it does nothing to resolve the problem.

Part of the difficulty here is that what is meant by 'good practice' depends largely upon the authorities you consult. Alexander, looking at this notion both in the literature and through empirical work with teachers, found four distinct, and possibly divergent, accounts of good practice:

1   This is a practice which I like, and which accords with my own personal philosophy of education.
2   This is a practice which works for me and which I feel most comfortable with.
3   This is a practice which I can prove is effective in enabling children to learn.
4   This is a practice which I (or others) expect to see, and it should therefore be adopted.

(ibid., p. 179)

Alexander is extremely sceptical, rightly we think, about the first and last statements above. These seem to be statements of mere personal or political preference which do not engage directly – or at all – with the proper purpose, scope, content or outcome of education. Points 2 and 3 seem better. In points 2 and 3 there is at least an implicit reference to educational ends and some concern for the effective realisation of such ends. In point 3 both the end, i.e. children's learning, and the means, i.e. what is effective, are explicit. But even here the formulation of the statement is extremely schematic. We are not told, for instance, what is the supposed content of this end and therefore we have no way of knowing whether the learning involved is worthwhile or not. And the implications of Alexander's argument here are surely correct. We can make no assessment of what is good practice, what constitutes effective teaching, independently of knowing the purposes that the education on offer is supposed to serve and the content of such an education. Aims determine means and without discussion of the former we can have no sensible discussion of the latter.

A test case

We can illustrate the points made above by going back to our History teacher's problem. It might be thought that what is at stake here is the best way to realise a single end, e.g. the best way for pupils to come to understand, say, the French Revolution. And this *might* be the question. But crucially it might not be. So, for instance, the teacher involved might choose the second method of teaching not because it is a better, or equally good, way of teaching about the French Revolution but, rather, because it is thought to realise educational ends which are not realised in the first method. So, for instance, this teacher's aim for education might be that the children have first-hand experience of historical documents, that their learning is self-directed, that it includes a large amount of discussion with their peers and that they reach their own conclusions. And it might be the case that these aims are taken to be as important, or more important, than learning facts about the French Revolution. If this is the case, then it has obvious implications for the method of teaching chosen because what looks inefficient from a certain point of view may be very efficient from a different point of view. We have posed these alternatives rather starkly here to show the type of misunderstandings that may occur. What is more likely is a situation in which the learning of historical facts is an aim for teachers adopting either methodology but, with the first methodology it is the overarching aim, whereas with the second, it is one aim among others.

It is worth pointing out in the context of this chapter that such a discussion of aims has its proper place within decisions about the curriculum and it should not suddenly surface at the level of debate about methodologies. Let us assume, at least for our present purposes, that we can reach agreement concerning educational aims. Where does this leave us with regard to the efficient realisation of such aims that should be at the heart of good practice? Given that we are now simply talking about a factual matter, i.e. what is an efficient method for realising this aim, we would expect that any claims about efficiency be suggested by empirical evidence. So, to return to Alexander's two favoured statements, the most likely claim is probably a version of statement 2 where 'it works for me' is couched in terms of success for the pupils at some agreed educational task, e.g. some exam or simply some successfully negotiated task. In the terms of our example, then the pupils do end up knowing about the French Revolution!

What about the stronger form of statement where we can talk about *proving* that a practice enables children to learn? The implied generality of this claim seems to go beyond mere personal experience. In order to support such a claim some reference would have to be made to evidence taken from not simply the experience of a single teacher but from the experience of teachers in general. And there may be great difficulties in getting such evidence. For instance, in a survey of empirical educational research in 1998 (Tooley and Darby 1998, p. 6), it was found that much of this research did not satisfy the elementary norms of good research practice (we shall return to this at the end of the chapter). In a book dealing with such research, *Giving Teaching Back to Teachers* (1984), Robin Barrow demonstrates at length that much of the empirical research of the time was conceptually muddled, lacking in educational judgement and structurally flawed. These negative findings mean that anyone seeking information concerning good practice from such research has to proceed with caution, and probably, the first sign of such caution is to realise that what is being sought here is never going to constitute the *proof* referred to in Alexander's third statement. The most that we can reasonably expect is some evidence that claims concerning good practice are true. We can surely hope that this more modest search might bear fruit. While for the majority of his book Barrow does not seem to deny the reasonableness of such an expectation, in some places he seems to argue that even this modest enquiry *must* be doomed to failure. So, for instance, he says (ibid., p. 186), 'The teacher should never act on a generalisation.' This sweeping denial of the very possibility of empirical research being fruitful is supported by an earlier argument. This argument, if it is sound, would prove that meaningful empirical educational research is impossible and therefore can produce no evidence whatsoever concerning good practice. The argument is both bold and important and its essential points are simple. In any real educational situation, according to Barrow, we are faced with multiple factors which might influence the outcome of the situation (boundary conditions). These are factors to do with the backgrounds of the children, the teacher's character, the ethos of the school, the relationships between children, etc. We may be able to control some of these variables but it is never likely that we can control all of them and we certainly cannot control all of the possible interactions between the different variables. But this means that any real educational situation is, in an important sense, unique, and if this is so, then it is simply impossible to generalise from such a situation (ibid., pp. 153–154). There is also a rich irony in Barrow's conclusion. On the basis of a few examples of empirical research he draws a general conclusion to the effect that teachers should never act on a generalisation. But this statement is itself a bold generalisation and, on his own account, no teacher should believe it. Barrow's thesis would seem, then, to be self-refuting, even if he could successfully draw the conclusion that he wants. But we do not think that he can because he does something that he criticises empirical researchers for doing, namely, making a bold generalisation on the basis of a very limited empirical base. More generally, any statement to the effect that all generalisations are false is paradoxical. If it is true, then there is at least one generalisation (itself) that is true and so the statement is false. On the other hand, if it is false then at least one generalisation (itself) must be true. We can conclude, therefore, that one should refrain from making statements to the effect that generalisations must be false.

Is each educational situation unique?

Now it might be replied that it is all very well pointing out that a lot of research is inadequate. This does not mean that it is possible to do good research. It might be, for example, that each educational situation is unique and that it is impossible to generalise from one situation to another. So, for example, when we have identified a school that enables its students to progress rapidly, there will be so many particular features of the situation in which this occurs, so that it will be impossible to generalise to other situations from this one. This seems to be a rehash of the earlier objection concerning boundary conditions, but one might say that these boundary conditions have far more importance in educational research. For example, the progress that students make in English in Year 8 might simply be due to the unique personal characteristics of Miss Jones who taught English in that class during the period of the research. Since the unique personality and teaching style of Miss Jones cannot be reproduced exactly anywhere else, it would be quite wrong to draw conclusions about other teachers and schools from the work of Miss Jones.

Before we go any further we need to pause and ask ourselves just what is being claimed here. It seems that there is more than one claim lying behind this objection. First, the claim might be that there is simply no fact of the matter that Miss Jones' teaching enables her students to progress, nor any fact of the matter that it does not enable her students to progress. Not only can we not *know* whether there is any fact that either it does or it does not, but that there *are* no such facts. This seems most unlikely. We would normally suppose that if Miss Jones tried to teach while drunk or if she read the newspaper instead of instructing her students and marking their work, that they would progress less well than if she had been attending to her duties. If we didn't have justified beliefs of this kind, then we would be totally indifferent to what kind of teaching or lack of it went on in classrooms. Since we are not totally indifferent, it is likely that we believe that there are such facts.

Someone might object that it is nothing more than common sense to suppose that drunken or newspaper-reading teachers do not enable their pupils to progress; we do not need educational research to tell us this. We shall return to the issue of common sense in due course, but this objection concedes one important point, namely that it *does* make a difference to learning what teachers do in the classroom, therefore there *are* facts about what enables students to progress and what does not.

Our objector might concede this but go on to say that, apart from what common sense tells us, there is nothing that we can usefully know about these issues from research. But this is scarcely an improvement. We could observe Miss Jones teaching while drunk and notice that she forgot her notes, failed to notice the time, departed from the syllabus and spoke in a slurred and unintelligible manner. Are we to say that we cannot *know* that poor learning in this instance is associated with the absence of notes, poor timekeeping, straying from the point and unintelligible attempts to communicate? This seems to be a very bold and implausible claim to make. Nor can the opponent of research claim that these features of Miss Jones' teaching are unique to Miss Jones and not to be found elsewhere. If we make the unhappy and unlikely assumption that there are many drunken teachers in our education system, we could investigate their performance and identify the features of drunken teaching that tend to detract from student learning. It is reasonable to suppose that common patterns of incompetence will emerge whoever the teachers are, although it is unlikely that exactly the same sequence of events will be repeated within each classroom. But this fact should not lead us to conclude that we can never learn anything about the characteristics of drunken teaching, merely that we should look for the common characteristics of it in different circumstances. It would be a brave anti-researcher who took the view either that we cannot know that drunkenness makes no difference to a teacher's ability, or that it does make a negative difference is merely a matter of common sense and cannot be further investigated.

This example might seem frivolous. So let us use another one from the literature. Much psychological research into learning and educational achievement has tried to show that there are invariant genetic factors that limit what it is possible for any given individual to achieve in their education. It is claimed that each individual has a genetic endowment of intelligence which cannot be altered and which sets limits to what he can learn (Galton 1892; Herrnstein 1996; Burt 1949). Now this claim is either true or false, so there are facts that will determine the truth of such claims. But is it common sense that it is either true or false? One can imagine, say, a racist saying that it is common sense that black people have low intelligence and fail to profit from school, while a liberal will claim the contrary view is common sense. Who is to decide between these two versions of common sense?

But if common sense is no guide, do we simply hold up our hands and say we can never *know* whether some groups of students are so unintelligent that they will fail to profit very much from schooling? Let us suppose that liberal common sense determines the answer. Then the claim that each individual has a genetic endowment of intelligence which cannot be altered and which sets limits to what he or she can learn is false. So we do know something very important about educability which should have a profound effect on the way in which we carry out education. We will not be inclined to test students for intelligence and to prescribe their teaching methods and curriculum accordingly. We will alter our expectations of what is possible for students who might otherwise have certain possibilities closed to them. More generally, we will not limit our expectations of student progress according to ideas about innate fixed intelligence. This would make a huge difference to any education system, that previously worked on the assumption that intelligence was innate and invariant, such as that of the UK until the post-war period (Gordon 1981; Winch 1990).

Nevertheless, we might still feel uneasy. After all, common sense is not something fixed. Until the nineteenth century it was common sense to think that God created the world and living creatures in seven days. In the early twenty-first century it is common sense in many parts of the world to believe that life evolved as a result of billions of years of causally regulated natural selection, in which God played no direct role. This example is particularly interesting since there are clearly rival ideas about what is common sense that are still in competition with each other, for instance in the United States. Shouldn't we go further and see what the evidence is for holding a belief in natural selection, on the one hand, and divine creation, on the other? After all, if common sense changed and creationism once again became common sense, should we just say, 'Ah, well, it's now common sense to believe in creationism so that's what we should do.' This seems to be an unsatisfactory response. Rational people generally want to have good reasons for believing what they believe. Good reasons are very often based on evidence. Beliefs about educability, such as the ones that we have just discussed, seem to be sensitive to evidence. For example, although it may be a difficult and complex process, we can come to learn whether or not it is likely that there is such a thing as general intelligence that determines all our abilities, whether ability is largely determined by genetic inheritance and whether certain abilities are more prevalent in some groups rather than in others. Admittedly, in this case we may also need to get clear about what we mean by 'intelligence' and findings may be disputed by different parties. But this means that the parties in dispute do believe that there is a truth of the matter and that it is possible to arrive at a conclusion about it. Otherwise they would not bother to carry out such investigations.

The normative theory of teaching

Our opponent of educational research may try a last throw. 'Teaching,' he will say, 'is a moral activity and, as such, is governed by moral norms, not by empirical facts.' 'What makes teaching good or bad is its conformity to moral norms, not whether some researcher has discovered an efficacious method of teaching. Therefore, empirical research has no bearing on what makes a teacher a good or bad teacher' (see Carr 2003, for an argument roughly along these lines). What teachers really need to know on this account, is how to conduct themselves in a morally appropriate manner, not what technical theories are effective in promoting learning. The main problem with this argument is its premise. Teaching does have to conform to moral norms, this *is* partly constitutive of good teaching. It is not true, however, that conformity to such norms, whether they are seen in terms of duties or of virtues possessed by morally mature individuals, is *wholly* constitutive of good teaching.

One of the reasons why we disapprove of teachers being drunk in the classroom or in public is that they set a bad example to students, whom we don't wish to encourage to become drunks. But we might also say that teaching while drunk is wrong because it makes one an ineffective teacher who cannot get students to learn what they are supposed to be learning. In other words, while we expect teachers to be moral exemplars, we also expect them to be effective in getting students to learn and this often means that teachers need to be able to instruct them appropriately and to know how to use effective means of classroom organisation. These are *technical* skills, given the end of getting students to learn X, we may ask what the most effective ways of doing this are. This does not mean that there are no moral constraints on what technical skills can be employed or on how they should be employed, any more than there are in any other occupation. It does mean, however, that teaching is not completely constituted by moral norms, it requires technical norms as well, of the form, 'If you want your students to learn X, then you should do Y.'

But our opponent might now claim triumphantly that this concedes the very point at issue. The statement 'If you want your students to learn X, then you should do Y' is a practical prescription, not a theoretical statement. As such, neither theories nor facts have any bearing on its validity. To spell this out a bit further, the claim is that this is an example of *practical* not *theoretical* reasoning. It is a simplified version of a general principle of the following kind:

> It is A's purpose to X.
> A understands that that Y-ing is a satisfactory way to X.
> A Ys.
>
> (Carr 1980, p. 59)

To take an example:

> It is A's purpose to act honestly.
> A understands that giving the money back to its owner is a satisfactory
> way of acting honestly.
> A hands the money back.

Why does A know that handing the money back is a satisfactory way of acting honestly? The answer is that a grasp of the concept of honesty involves appreciation of the fact that one should not retain possession of something that one does not own. This is partly constitutive of what it means to be honest. So the understanding that giving the money back to its owner is a satisfactory way of acting honestly is the grasp of a conceptual truth about the meaning of honesty. Likewise, it is A's purpose to act honestly, because acting honestly is constitutive of a worthwhile life and it is part of one's conceptual appreciation of the nature of morality that one should lead a worthwhile life to the best of one's ability. So one can understand that one should hand the money back as a result of reasoning about moral concepts, not through the knowledge of any particular state of affairs or empirical theory. If this is the general pattern of practical reasoning, which will govern the actions of teachers as well as other practitioners, then it seems as if no particular facts have any bearing on the conclusion. And if this is so, then empirical educational research, which purports to bring facts to bear on the determination of educational action, will be irrelevant to teachers' actions.

To evaluate this argument, let us look at a different argument of the same form.

> It is A's purpose to teach reading effectively to Year 2.
> A understands that using synthetic phonics is a satisfactory way to teach reading effectively to Year 2.
> A uses synthetic phonics.

This is the same kind of argument as the one about honesty above, but understanding that using synthetic phonics is a satisfactory way of teaching reading is *not* a conceptual accomplishment concerning what the nature of teaching reading is. Many would claim that synthetic phonics is actually harmful to getting children to learn to read. If the second premise of the above argument is true, then it is true *partly* because it is a morally acceptable way of teaching children to learn to read and partly because it has been shown to be *effective* in promoting children's learning. And the only way in which one could determine that aspect of its truth would be through investigation of its effectiveness through empirical studies.

So the fact that teaching, like any other occupation, is morally constrained does not mean that facts or empirical theories have no bearing on whether or not practice is effective. We need to find out whether or not synthetic phonics is effective before we can recommend it to teachers as something that they should use. There are various methods of investigation of such questions, involving the comparison of synthetic phonics with other methods in a variety of different settings and long-term evaluation of the effectiveness of different methods. The evaluation of this kind of research may take a long time and the results may incline us to believe that *on balance* the use of synthetic phonics is most suitable for *most* pupils in *most* circumstances. In other words, evaluation of the research might lead us to conclusions that indicate that using synthetic phonics is the best course of action among alternatives, rather than the only possible one. This means not only that educational researchers should approach their task with humility, understanding that arriving at conclusions may be a lengthy process and that certainty about one's rightness may not be a possible outcome in all cases, but also that teachers should acquaint themselves with research so that they can also form judgements as to the quality of what is being offered.

Conclusion: teachers and educational research

The fact that a lot of educational research does not measure up to such standards of quality is one reason why we should constantly try to improve it. Tooley and Darby's criteria of good practice (1998, p. 12) are a good, if minimal, starting point for a debate as to what should constitute good educational research. Their criteria for 'good practice' in empirical research are as follows:

1 Does the research involve triangulation in order to establish its trustworthiness?
2 Does the research avoid sampling bias?
3 Does the research use primary sources in the literature review?
4 Does the research avoid partisanship in the way it is carried out and in the interpretation of the data?

(Tooley and Darby also provide criteria for non-empirical research. These are interesting and worthwhile but not to our present purpose.)

The first criterion simply points to the fact that in researching an area of interest, e.g. with regard to sexism within promotion procedures, a researcher should not approach this from a single point of view, e.g. that of the person who alleges sexual discrimination, but should test this point of view by collecting evidence from everybody involved in such procedures, for instance, the head-teacher involved, the board of governors of the school, the person appointed and other people who have benefited or failed to benefit from such procedures. Only in this way can a researcher build up the type of impartial picture which can support worthwhile research findings.

The second criterion simply asks that we are shown, in the conduct and reporting of empirical research, how the sample used in the research was selected, so that we can decide whether such a sample is likely to be typical of the wider population. If we cannot know whether it is typical or not, we cannot generalise from the research situation to other situations.

With regard to the use of primary sources, researchers have a duty when, for instance, involved in a literature review, to match any reports of the work of others with the work itself. It is all too easy to simply cite reports that you happen to agree with, rather ensuring that such reports are, as a matter of fact, accurate.

The last criterion, regarding partisanship, does not involve the researcher being indifferent to the research and its results. Such an indifference would be the end of research in any meaningful sense. Rather, it involves researchers being aware that emotional, moral or political commitments may cloud judgements and that therefore measures should be in place, e.g. triangulation and fair sampling, which minimise such distortions of judgement.

None of these criteria are particularly difficult to understand and employ. And they do at least provide a starting point – if only that – for the evaluation of empirical educational research. Given that anyone entering the teaching profession is likely to have their professional lives constrained by the results of such research: either directly, because some minister, civil servant or headteacher knows of the research and has decided that this is the way they should proceed; or indirectly, because the results of such research, often detached from their original context, become the 'common sense' of some staffroom. Then it is of the utmost importance that teachers should be taught how to evaluate such research. Elsewhere in this book we have supported the notion of autonomy and a critical engagement with our culture. What we suggest here for teachers is merely another aspect of these themes.

This will mean, we suspect, that the teaching of empirical research within our departments of education will have to change. All too often in the past the 'results' of such research have been passed on uncritically to the people being taught. Indeed, years ago, we heard a colleague provide a summary of the work of Skinner, Piaget and Vygotsky to a class. Despite the fact that the findings of these three researchers are mutually contradictory and start from completely different assumptions from each other, he assured the class that all were true! Students of education must be given the tools to separate the good from the bad in educational research. Only in this way can we be confident of their judgement when they become the users of such research. And, as an added bonus, we suspect that the creation of a truly critical audience would rapidly lead to a decrease in the amount of bad research that is presently produced.

Questions for further discussion

1   What are the moral constraints on pedagogic practice?
2   Who should decide what pedagogy is appropriate?
3   'If Barrow is right, teachers could never accumulate useful experience.' Discuss.
4   Can practitioners ever learn from empirical theory?
5   How would you react if someone said that the evidence showed that you had to teach in a certain way?

Further reading

There are many 'how to teach' manuals which recommend various forms of 'good practice'. For an incisive conceptual analysis of the meanings of 'good practice' see Robin Alexander, *Policy and Practice in the Primary School* (London, Routledge, 1992), Chapter 11. Alexander's book is also an empirical study which is an object lesson on what can go wrong when ideas about good practice which do not depend on evidence are allowed to take control in an education authority. Recent scepticism about educational research can be found in David Carr, *Making Sense of Education* (London, Routledge, 2003), Chapter 4. For a balanced account of the possibilities and limitations of educational research, see Richard Pring, *The Philosophy of Educational Research* (London, Continuum, 2000). The best introduction to scientific research that we know is W.H. Newton-Smith, *The Rationality of Science* (London, Routledge, 1981).

Chapter 5

Standards, performance and assessment

This chapter considers what assessment is and whether it is educationally valuable. Various arguments against assessment are considered and rejected. These include: (1) the claim that education involves providing educational opportunities rather than knowledge; (2) the claim that serious teachers need only monitor rather than assess their pupils' progress; and (3) the claim that assessment can never be fully accurate and is thus generally misleading. Arguments in favour of assessment are developed in terms of the need for accountability and the claim, made in Chapter 3, that teaching involves the serious intention to get pupils to learn. The chapter goes on to look at whether or not educational performances can be compared in terms both of individual pupil progress and the relative success of schools or even nations. It is argued that such comparison can be made provided that one is careful to qualify one's findings in terms of possible margins of error.

Current concern with these issues: the National Curriculum, international competition and comparison

It would be difficult to identify an educational topic that receives more concern in contemporary societies than that of assessment. The growth of free trade since the Second World War and the competition between states that it has brought in its wake have focused the minds of governments on those factors that contribute to economic effectiveness. Rightly or wrongly, education is now widely thought to be a key determinant of economic success. Everyone wants a good 'return' from their investment in education in order to stay ahead or even to keep their place in global economic competition. On an individual level educational success brings the prospect of a well-paid job in a labour market where the unskilled have fewer opportunities.

At the same time the so-called 'culture of accountability' has grown in which those who receive resources for a particular purpose are called upon to justify their use of those resources. In education this has meant an increasing focus on educational performance, both at the level of the individual and of national educational achievement. But how is educational performance to be determined? Is it even possible to do so in a credible way? These are two questions which we will attempt to answer in this chapter. We will start from the concept of accountability, and then go on to look at the central concepts that are commonly used to describe and analyse educational performance, paying particular attention to assessment, which seems to us to be the central concept in the explanation of accountability. We will then go on to look at an important moral argument for the use of assessment and consider two objections to common forms of educational assessment, arguing that in the end they do not command conviction. We will then go on to look at the claim that educational progress in aggregate can be measured, so that one can, for instance, say that School A improves its pupils more than School B. We will conclude by appraising the scope and limitations of educational assessment.

Accountability: what it is and the different ways of securing it: process and outcome based

As we said, accountability can be defined as the idea that those who receive resources for a particular purpose can be called upon to justify their use of those resources. It is natural to think that this means that those who are given resources to provide education are expected, not only not to waste the resources provided, but to use them as effectively as possible. This means that they are expected to fulfil the aims of education by imparting knowledge, understanding and skill to pupils. This is a straightforward enough idea, but we need to look a little more closely at what it entails.

Education takes place through processes that involve learning and teaching. The point of having an education system is that people are enabled to learn. This is usually done through teaching or training them. As we saw in Chapters 2 and 3, the aims of a public education system relate to what its recipients should *know* as a result of educational processes. This seems like an obvious point but it is crucial for our understanding of the issue of accountability. Because the aims of education relate to what young people should know as a result of education, the criterion for whether those aims are achieved is whether or not young people do actually know what it is intended that they should know as a result of having had an educational experience. To the extent that they do know, educational aims are achieved. Clearly fulfilling educational aims is not an all-or-nothing matter. Some people may learn what it is intended that they should learn, others may not and any individual may learn the material more or less successfully. In order to determine whether or not educational aims are met, then it will be necessary to conduct an investigation as to what they have learned and how well they have learned it.

Obvious as all this may sound, there have been objections. It has been argued, for example, that what education provides is not education, but the delivery of educational opportunities (Tooley 1998). One may take it then, if this story is to be believed, that education is successful if it succeeds in delivering educational opportunities. However, one can deliver educational opportunities without the recipients of those opportunities learning anything. This model of the aims of education might conceivably work in a situation where a market in education was being provided to private customers who were then free to do what they liked with the opportunities provided. Arguably, if someone buys a car they buy the opportunity to make journeys, it is not the fault of the car salesman if they fail to take up these opportunities. Pursuing the analogy, if someone buys educational opportunities, then it is not the fault of the educator if they fail to take them up. We might just grant this, although it strains credulity. We do not know of many private schools that just offer their pupils the opportunity to learn. Possible exceptions might be those ultra-liberal establishments that deliberately avoid placing any pressure whatsoever on their pupils. However, few parents, having paid large amounts of money to educate their children, would be happy to be told, on hearing that their offspring had not learned anything at school, that they were, nevertheless, given ample opportunities to do so, but had failed to take them up. We can be reasonably confident, therefore, that most private schools and most parents paying to have their children educated in such establishments regard it as a criterion of success that children actually learn what they are supposed to learn (as set out in the school curriculum), rather than that they merely have opportunities to learn.

Public education systems do not normally couch their aims in terms of opportunities either. The reason is simple; education is funded by the public in order to secure an educated population, not a population that has had the opportunity to become educated.[1] If the government were only concerned about the latter, then they would not make education compulsory for a substantial number of years. As we saw in Chapter 1, education is too important for states to leave to chance in this way. So we are confident that education is funded principally by that state in order to educate children and young people and that the criterion of success is that they are actually educated, that is, that they learn what it is intended that they should learn. The requirement of accountability for public education systems is, then, the requirement that the money spent on education should be spent on achieving educational aims through young people's mastery of the content of the curriculum. This entails, we shall argue, that assessment plays a crucial role in ensuring accountability.

Some crucial notions: standards, performance, progression, assessment

What does assessment involve? Clearly, it involves the evaluation of learners' performances. But in order to do this it is necessary to have a criterion of success. If learners learn something but not enough, or if not enough learners learn enough, then it is natural to say that the aims of education have not been met or that they have only partly been met. We do not, therefore, just require learners to demonstrate that they have learned something, but that they have learned what they are supposed to have learned. In other words, we need a standard against which to judge their performance in learning (Pring 1992). A standard, then, is a kind of educational measuring rod against which learning performance can be measured. Thus, to take an example from the English National Curriculum, at Key Stage 1 in English, *Reading*, pupils should demonstrate phonemic awareness and phonic knowledge. Specifically, they should be able to do the following:

1   Hear, identify, segment and blend phonemes in words.
2   Sound and name the letters of the alphabet.
3   Link sound and letter patterns, exploring rhyme, alliteration and other sound patterns.
4   Identify syllables in words.
5   Recognise that the same sounds may have different spellings and that the same spellings may relate to different sounds.

(DfEE 1999, p. 46)

These statements are the *standards* appropriate to a pupil attaining Key Stage 1 in reading within the English segment of the National Curriculum. It is natural that pupils, parents, schools, the government and the public should want to know how well these standards have been met. Richard Pring has drawn attention to an important potential confusion here (Pring 1992). The term 'standards' as it is commonly used in assessment contexts is ambiguous. What is actually produced is, strictly speaking, the educational *performance*. The means by which the performance is assessed are the relevant educational *standards*. It is common to hear talk about standards rising and falling when what is actually *meant* is that educational performances are rising or falling or are better or worse than other educational performances. The *standard*, strictly speaking, is the criterion or measuring rod against which the performances are judged. Naturally, pupils and parents will be interested in their own performance. Parents and schools will be interested in the performance of schools. Local Education Authorities will be interested in the performance of the schools that are their responsibility and the public and government will be interested in the performance of the education system as a whole. In order to find out what that *performance* is, in a way that can satisfy the wishes of all these parties, one must first assess the performance of individual pupils to see whether, and to what extent, the statement setting out the standards which learners are meant to achieve, is actually being met. Assessment is the procedure which is used to do this. Pupils are asked to demonstrate their knowledge which is then checked against the appropriate *standard*. This is what is generally meant by the term 'assessment'.

Progression

When we ask how well a pupil is doing or how effective a school is, we are usually concerned with educational *progress*. The idea of educational progress is that, between two times, pupils learn so that by the second time, they know more than they did at the first time. The more they know, the greater their progress. A little reflection shows that one cannot measure progress without assessing. In order to show to what extent a pupil has progressed between two times, t1 and t2, it is necessary to measure their educational performance at t1 and then again at t2. The greater the difference in knowledge that there is between these two times, the greater the progress made by the pupil.

This sounds obvious, but as with so many matters in education, matters are not so simple. In the first place, it is relatively easy to tell whether or not an individual pupil has progressed by the method mentioned. But we usually want to know more than this. For instance, we would like to know the extent to which the school has contributed to the growth in the pupils' knowledge. Merely knowing the results of assessment at the end of a given school year is not going to give us much help in this. Scores at the end of compulsory schooling in one school may look very impressive compared to those of other schools, but if they actually reflect the fact that pupils already arrived at the school knowing a great deal, and in fact have progressed little beyond that point, then that may reflect very badly on a school. It is no good reflection on a school's effectiveness, either, if a pupil has learned a lot over, say, a year, but all the learning has taken place thanks to a private tutor that the parents hired outside school hours. Or, to take another case, if pupils have to battle against all kinds of adverse circumstances: poverty, no room to study, adverse peer pressure, and so on, it is not necessarily all to the discredit of the school that they failed to make pupils progress very much.

It is clear that actually measuring the effect of a school on pupil progress may not be as simple as it appears at first sight. The reason is that pupil progress is affected by a huge number of factors, relatively few of which are within the control of schools. Since one can only assign praise or blame according to whether or not a person or institution is responsible for the processes that led to an outcome, it follows that we can only judge schools according to those factors for which they are responsible. Since they are not responsible for the social class of pupils or their achievement before they arrive at school, or the nature of the communities from which the children come, and these are potentially very significant factors determining educational outcomes, it follows that there may be a number of very important factors affecting pupil progress which are outside the control of individual schools.

Assessment: the Flew argument from seriousness

We will look at one argument that casts doubt on the idea that one can make comparisons between assessments conducted at widely different times and places and suggest that this argument is not convincing. However, we need to ask whether there are more compelling reasons to engage in assessment. There is an argument, thanks to Anthony Flew, which suggests that there is. Flew's argument (which we state in our own words) goes as follows (see Flew 1976). Education is an activity that can be conducted well or badly. One major criterion of success in an educational activity is that those to whom it is directed learn what it is intended that they should learn. In order to find out whether or not someone has learned what it is intended that they should learn, one needs to assess their knowledge to see whether or not it incorporates what was intended by their teachers that they should learn as a result of the process of education. Those who are serious about what they are doing will invariably take steps to find out whether or not they are being successful in what they are doing and, if so, to what degree. Assessment is the measure of success in education. Therefore, if educators are serious about what they are doing, they will assess their students.

On this argument, assessment is a central feature of any educational process that is seriously conducted. If Flew's argument is sound, educators must see assessment as a central feature of their business. Note that Flew's argument only shows that educators need to assess their pupils' performance. It does not show that there should be public examinations, league tables of school performances or any of the other apparatus of modern accountability in education. However, if Flew's argument is wrong, then there is no point in all the other activities, since they all depend on data aggregated from the level of pupil achievement. Note also that Flew's argument does not require that assessment be *perfect*. In order to fulfil his requirement, it neither has to assess everything that the pupil learns, nor does it have to be completely error-free in its procedures and results. The requirement is, essentially, that assessment should both be conducted where it is feasible and necessary to do so and that it should be as error-free and as comprehensive as possible, given constraints of time, resources and testing procedures. Perfection is not available in this fallen world.

One final point about Flew's argument, which is not always noted, should be made. In order to establish the success of an activity, one needs *criteria* of when one is or is not successful and to what extent. Therefore, in order to fulfil Flew's requirement of seriousness, one would have to employ criteria within the assessment process which would establish whether or not the educational activity was successful and to what extent. This type of assessment is usually known as *criterion referenced assessment* and is usually contrasted with assessment that simply records achievement and rank orders the pupils according to the degree of their achievement. Success or failure is then determined at some arbitrary cut-off point in the range of scores. But unless the scores are tied to criteria that determine what has been learned, they tell the assessor no more than who has done better than whom in the assessment process. It follows from Flew's own argument that this will be insufficient to establish success relative to what should have been learned.

White (1999) has argued that Flew's argument only shows that teachers should *monitor* pupils' progress, not assess it. By this he means that the teacher needs to take account of what a learner's responses reveal and does not need any further action on the teacher's part (ibid., p. 205). This response could include the 'rapt look on their faces' or the question that they ask the teacher. Therefore, the setting of assignments, tests and exams is unnecessary for a teacher who is serious about what they are doing. We do not find this convincing. Teachers who want to know whether or not they have been successful need to know whether a statement like 'A knows that p' where 'A' stands for a pupil and 'p' for a piece of knowledge is true or false. A rapt look or a penetrating question cannot tell them that. Pupils who do not ask questions or who do not look rapt will either be judged wrongly or not at all. Serious teachers will not leave matters to chance in such a way, but will devise systematic and fair ways of investigating what pupils have learned and thus to establish whether statements of the form 'A knows that p' are true or false. One may call these 'monitoring' if one likes, but to all intents and purposes, it is the same as assessment.

Arguments against assessment: validity is a problem

These points, although obvious enough, need to be stated since the very idea of criterion-referenced assessment has come under attack from some philosophical commentators. Andrew Davis (1995, 1998) has mounted a sustained attack on criterion-referenced assessment, although his later writings (Davis 1999; Davis and White 2001) have qualified the position somewhat. The basis of Davis's criticism is that criterion-referenced assessment can never be valid in the sense that it can never accurately measure what it sets out to measure, namely knowledge acquired by a learner. As we have seen, assessment is related to particular performances, usually in the form of tests or exams. The problem with these formalised systems of measuring performance is that they are unable to capture knowledge in an adequate sense. Davis argues that genuinely valuable knowledge is what he calls 'rich knowledge (Davis 1995) which has the characteristic of being (1) connected with other items of knowledge in the knower's mind; and (2) capable of manifestation in a variety of forms in a variety of circumstances. Since the assessment of performance, by its nature concentrates on *isolating* items of knowledge from others for assessment purposes and on asking pupils to demonstrate their knowledge *in a particular way*, all that it can hope to assess is 'thin' or 'procedural' knowledge that is both isolated and manifested in a narrow and restricted way. It cannot hope to capture the nature of the rich knowledge which, if education has been properly conducted, will be the kind of knowledge which the pupil has acquired.

Conventional assessment may well be *reliable*, that is, one may obtain the same result on repeated occasions, but it will not be valid, it will not measure what it aims to measure. On the other hand, to attempt to assess rich knowledge, its connectedness and the various ways in which it is manifested will mean that we will need a variety of assessment techniques in order to capture its different dimensions. If we do this, we will necessarily obtain different results with different assessment instruments and will therefore sacrifice *reliability* in the quest for validity. Davis is careful to say, in later publications, that assessment does have a limited function. It can, for example, give teachers a profile of individual pupil performance and can allow schools to gain a picture of aggregate pupil progress (Davis 1999). What it cannot do is to serve as an instrument by which one could compare the performances of different schools or the performance of a public education system as a whole.

We have already noted some of the difficulties involved in measuring progress and we shall return to these in the discussion of school effectiveness. However, the points raised by Davis need to be addressed before we can go into these issues. First, it has to be acknowledged that no assessment system is perfect and that there is invariably a trade-off to be made between validity and reliability. The critical question here may not be as Davis claims, a matter of rich knowledge, but 'Are the assessment instruments fit for purpose?' So, for instance, to refer back to the Attainment Targets for Key Stage 1 *Reading* in the English National Curriculum, are the items mentioned worth assessing, and is it possible to devise realistic methods of assessment? If they have to be capable of measuring *every* dimension of pupil knowledge, then they will never be fit for purpose in this sense. But we must be realistic and not expect too much from assessment systems. Second, though, given this reservation, Davis's critique seriously misunderstands the nature of assessment. To engage in criterion-referenced assessment is not to misunderstand the interconnected and multidimensional nature of knowledge but to make an attempt to capture it. Assessment can be badly carried out. One way which this can happen is when the precise way in which the assessment will be carried out is known by teachers and pupils. In these circumstances, especially when the outcomes of assessment processes are of some significance, there will be a great temptation for teachers to teach in such a way that performance on the assessment instrument will be maximised, irrespective of the knowledge targets set out in the curriculum.

However, assessment, when it is properly administered, is meant to *sample* the knowledge gained by the pupils. In the above example, we could not expect assessment to test whether a child could identify every syllable in every word, rather, we expect realistic assessment to test whether children can do this with words which they may reasonably be expected to encounter and from their success or failure at this test we infer a general ability. The idea is that the pupils learn the matter in the curriculum which, if it is properly taught, will have the connected and multidimensional character that Davis argues that useful knowledge has. However, because of its complex nature, no assessment procedure could, in the space of a small number of tests, adequately capture all of this. However, by formulating questions that bring out different aspects of a pupil's knowledge, the assessor will gain a reasonably accurate picture of how well the subject matter as a whole is grasped. This will be done by sampling the pupil's knowledge, both in respect of its factual, practical or inferential content and by doing so in such a way that the connectedness of that knowledge is also sampled. Just as the voting intentions of a population can be gauged by asking a representative sample of voters how they intend to vote, so the knowledge of students can be gauged by sampling their knowledge.

Behind the apparent negative thinking and unwarranted scepticism that lies behind this critique of assessment, there lies, however, a serious issue. Assessment is the means to an end, that of forming a reasonably accurate picture of what pupils have learned. As a *means* it should be subordinated to the *end* of forming this picture. The main aim of teaching and learning is to promote learning, not for students to do well in assessments. *Formative* assessment, which is used to understand the level of pupil performance and to identify strengths and weaknesses, is a proper part of the teacher's armoury of techniques in promoting teaching and learning, and, as Flew's argument demonstrates, is necessary if teachers are serious about teaching. This kind of assessment is part and parcel of everyday teaching and learning.

Summative assessment, on the other hand, is concerned with certification, with regulating entry to employment, to further study and to the maintenance of accountability. Understandably, success in summative assessment is of great concern to all involved: pupils and students, teachers, parents, education authorities and the government. It is important that the processes of summative assessment are kept distinct from those of teaching and learning. Otherwise there is a danger that the curriculum will become distorted by the assessment items. Since assessment is meant to provide a *comprehensive* as well as an accurate picture of what has been learned, the teaching of only those items that it is known will be assessed will inevitably subvert this process. It is essential that the curriculum covered is that which will be sampled for assessment processes. But if only those items are taught which it is known will be assessed, the curriculum will be impoverished. It is very often stated that it is wrong to 'teach to the test'. In one sense there is nothing wrong with this, if by it one means simply that the curriculum that is to be assessed is properly covered in the teaching programme. It is wrong in those cases where comprehensiveness is sacrificed to the goal of doing well in summative assessment.

No assessment can be perfect. There have to be compromises between reliability and validity, and validity can never be 100 per cent. There will always be, as Dearden (1979) pointed out, an inferential gap between assessment performance and pupil knowledge. We have to be satisfied that assessment is as fair and as accurate as possible. It is worth pointing out, however, that most human knowledge is imperfect and incomplete and our knowledge of what pupils know will always be so. This is not a reason for dispensing altogether with summative assessment. It is an argument for taking it seriously, designing and administering it carefully and for keeping it under review.

Comparability of standards: performance against standards

So far we have argued that, given a standard, it is possible to measure performance against that standard. Obviously it is very interesting and important for parents, schools and children to be able to see how well performance is being achieved against a given standard (such as the example given above). For the purposes of comparison and accountability, particularly of the public education system as a whole with either previous performance or with the performance of other education systems, it is necessary to use the same standard against which to compare performances. Failing this, we need to be able to compare standards with one another. There are two problems that need to be addressed. First, it is unlikely that any two education systems will use the same standards for assessment. For example, the UK and France will have different pupil expectations at different stages and in some areas, the standards expected will be widely divergent. We would not expect, for example, a 12-year-old British child to achieve the same degree of proficiency in French as his or her 12-year-old French counterpart. Second, if we wish to compare current performances with those achieved in the past, it is necessary that they are compared against a common standard.

What, however, if we cannot compare diverse performances against a common standard? If this is true, the use of assessments to compare historically distant performances with current ones, or to compare performances in other education systems with our own would not be possible and the role of assessment would be severely limited. How worried should we be by this possibility? We should be worried if it is not possible to compare standards with one another. One reason why this might be so is if, in comparing standards A and B, we need a further standard C against which to judge them. It might then seem that, in order to compare A and B with C, we need a further standard D with which to compare these three and so on, *ad infinitum*. If this argument (set out in Pring 1992) is valid, then it is logically impossible to compare one educational standard with another.

We do not, however, think that this is a valid argument and, consequently, we do not think that there is a logical difficulty in comparing standards. Let us illustrate this point with an example. The criteria for reading given above are the relevant standard for children of, say 7 years of age. If we were to say that this should be the standard for 8-year-olds rather than 7-year-olds, then, given the reasonable assumption that more knowledge is to be expected from 8-year-olds rather than 7-year-olds, it would be correct to say that the standard is now lower because we assume that 7-year-olds now have to accomplish less. All we need to appeal to here is the principle that older children should be expected to know more about a subject than younger children. Once again, making use of the reasonable principle that a standard that requires less knowledge than another standard, alike in all other respects, is a lower standard, we can say that the same criteria applied to 8-year-olds constitute a lower standard than if the criteria are applied to 7-year-olds, since 8-year-olds should know more than 7-year-olds. So there is no problem in principle about saying that one standard is higher or lower than another.

Nevertheless, there may still be technical difficulties in comparing standards, which we will now look at. These are of two sorts: those that relate to comparisons across different education systems at the same time and those that relate to historical comparisons within an education system. The first problem is one that the designers of international comparative studies, such as TIMMS (an international maths test) and PISA (an international test of a range of subjects) have to grapple with. The problem here should be fairly clear. One can construct a standard *within* an education system that allows you to compare the performance of pupils within that system. How, though, is it possible to compare two or more systems each with their own internal standards? For example, to 'recognise that the same sounds may have different spellings and that the same spellings may relate to different sounds' may be an expectation for 7-year-olds in one education system and for 8-year-olds in another. More worryingly, some spelling systems such as English may be more irregular and harder to master than others, such as French, so the achievement of what is nominally the same standard may just be harder for an English pupil than it is for a French one. The solution to such difficulties involves the construction of an independent standard, which can be applied to pupils of the same age in all the education systems in which the comparison takes place. In the case of reading, this would mean that one would have to construct a test of the same level of difficulty for each language and as nearly equivalent as possible as a text. This difficulty is not insurmountable, provided one accepts that one can never achieve perfection in assessment. But, as we have argued already, it is not the goal of assessment to achieve perfection.

This can also be illustrated with an example from the National Curriculum. At the end of Key Stage 2 (roughly 11 years of age) pupils should be able to do the following in relation to understanding texts:

1   Use inference and deduction.
2   Look for meaning beyond the literal.
3   Make connections between different parts of a text.
4   Use their knowledge of other texts that they have read.

(DfEE 1999, p. 53)

International comparisons can be made by testing such abilities through the use of texts at the same level of difficulty, which itself can be specified by a tighter definition of the four criteria above appropriate to the age of the pupils being assessed.

Historical comparisons are especially difficult the further one goes back. For comparison with the recent past, one can use the same test repeatedly. The further back one goes, the less valid a previous test is likely to be. To take a reading test as an example, common vocabulary may have changed (e.g. 'lorry' for 'truck'), and the underlying level of achievement may have increased or decreased. This is a problem because tests are usually standardised to ensure a normal 'bell-shaped curve' pattern of achievement. Periodic restandardisation means that test results before and after this has happened are not directly comparable. As we go further back, we will find that reading tests in the past measure different aspects of reading to those that are currently measured, and that even further back there are no tests at all. The critical point is, though, that it should be possible to compare performances year on year and nothing that we have said about the difficulty of longer-term comparisons has a serious bearing on that.

Progression and value added

Progression, as we have seen, involves measuring the increase of pupil knowledge over a period. When we are interested in evaluating how well an education system is performing, the fairest way of doing so would seem to be by evaluating the progress made by pupils. In terms of the previous discussion, it will be necessary to calculate the progression between assessment periods and then aggregate them, first for classes, then for schools, then for education authorities and finally for a nation as a whole. Unfortunately, there are difficulties. First, as we have already noted, there are a number of factors for which the school is not responsible, which have an important effect on pupil progress. Second, there are error factors which force us to treat any progression data as subject to a margin of error. These errors arise from a number of sources: first, pupil performance fluctuates from year to year dependent on the individual abilities of pupils; second, where there is frequent movement of pupils to and from a school, it is difficult to gather accurate data for the school as a whole; third, there are factors that have caused pupils to learn outside the school or which have caused pupils to forget what they have learned. Finally, since we know that factors such as poverty, sex of pupils and social background have an important effect on pupil progress, they need to be taken into account when calculating the effectiveness of the school as a whole. Since such factors cannot be precisely measured, but must be estimated, there is further scope for error in the assessment of a school's contribution to pupil progress.

This means that we must be very cautious in assessing school effectiveness, or the extent to which schools promote pupil progress. The margins of error in estimating effectiveness will be so great that it is probably impossible to make any meaningful comparisons between schools with the same background factors that achieve different, although similar, rates of progression. Minor differences between schools may be so small that they can be accounted for by chance factors and measurement error. It is more likely that we will be able to draw meaningful conclusions in situations where there are widely differing rates of progress and where the background factors of the schools are very similar. This means that we will really only be able to make secure judgements in relation to schools performing at the best or worst extremes of possible effectiveness. This might, however, be a valuable exercise if it enabled schools and policy-makers to identify factors that tended to promote or retard progress. It would be tempting to disavow all such attempts as too subject to error to be really meaningful. We would oppose such a judgement for the following reason.

Let us suppose the contrary, that the way a school organises itself makes no difference whatsoever to the rate of progression of pupils. That is an empirical supposition and, as such, is either true or false. If it is either true or false, then there are facts of the matter which make it true or false and which can, in principle be investigated. If the supposition is true, then we have discovered that there is such a thing as school effectiveness. If the supposition is false, then we have discovered that there is no such thing. Either way, the question cannot be decided through reasoning alone, but must be determined through investigation, however difficult this turns out to be. The alternatives seem to be either to say that there are no facts that would determine whether some schools are more effective than others, which seems absurd, or one says that it is quite alright to have no beliefs one way or the other concerning school effectiveness. In the first instance we would be committed to saying that, for example, the fact that School A was wholly staffed by brilliant, well-qualified teachers and School B was staffed by itinerant back-packers with minimal qualifications could, as a matter of logic, have no bearing on the fact that School A pupils apparently made more progress than those in School B. In the second instance, we would have to say that teachers, pupils, parents and policy-makers would be justified in having no opinion on whether say, good teaching or good school organisation had an effect on pupil progress. This is scarcely better, as it suggests a complete abdication of responsibility for investigating something of great importance and relevance to learning in schools. We should conclude therefore that, however daunting the difficulties in investigating the matter and however tentative the conclusions that we might draw from such investigations, a refusal to engage in such an investigation is based either on a denial that there are facts that might determine the matter or on the assumption that it is justifiable not to have an opinion on the matter one way or the other.

Conclusion: what can assessment tell us and what does it not tell us?

1   We have argued for and defended the view that teaching requires assessment if it is to be taken seriously. We have defended this view against sceptical challenges and, in doing so, have acknowledged that assessment can never be perfect.

2   Accountability in education requires that there be assessment. What successful education offers is knowledge, not the opportunity to acquire

knowledge. Serious teachers will assess their pupils and this requires that they have at their disposal fair and reasonably thorough ways of determining what their pupils have learned.

3   It is important to distinguish between performances and standards. Standards can be compared with each other both historically and between different countries. It is therefore possible to make international comparisons of educational performance between different countries by using a common standard to measure performances in different countries.

Questions for further discussion

1   What steps should teachers take to ensure that they are being successful?
2   Does it matter if assessment is imperfect?
3   Can international comparisons of educational performance tell us anything useful?
4   'Standards have definitely declined, British education is nothing like it was before the war.' Can a statement like this be assessed for its truth or falsity?
5   Are exams ever necessary for assessment purposes?

Further reading

Andrew Davis's *The Limits of Educational Assessment* (Oxford, Blackwell, 1998) is the only sustained philosophical critique of assessment policy that we know of. His *Educational Assessment: A Critique of Current Policy* (London, Philosophy of Education Society of Great Britain, 1999) is a more accessible introduction to his ideas. Anthony Flew's argument for assessment can be found in his *Sociology, Equality and Education* (London, Macmillan, 1976). Another writer who has tried to defend assessment practices is Kevin Williams in 'Assessment and the Challenge of Scepticism' in David Carr (ed.), *Education, Knowledge and Truth* (London, Routledge, 1998). Pring's distinction between standards and performances is to be found in his article 'Standards and Quality in Education', *British Journal of Educational Studies*, 40, 3: 4–22 (1992). Winch discusses this in 'In Defence of Educational Standards', in his *Quality and Education* (Oxford, Blackwell, 1996). On international comparisons, see Harvey Goldstein, *Interpreting International Comparisons of Student Achievement* (Paris, UNESCO, 1995). On the interpretation of value-added data in the UK, see Harvey Goldstein *et al.*, *The Use of Value Added Information in Judging School Performance* (London, Institute of Education, 2000).

Chapter 6

Moral, personal and civic education

In this chapter we look at three important but relatively neglected aspects of education. Moral education is concerned not only with the development of right conduct and attitudes, but also with understanding of moral issues. In the context of a plural society it is also concerned with accommodation to moral beliefs that are not one's own. Moral education is thus concerned, not only with what one should do and what attitudes one should take to other people, but also with understanding why people act and behave as they do, and with understanding the beliefs that they have. Personal education is concerned with how one gets on with other people in order to do what one wants to do in life. The relationship between personal and moral education is explained and some indication is given of the possible content and methods of personal education. Finally, we look at civic education and consider the knowledge and skill that meaningful citizenship involves. We consider and reject various objections to civic education and go on to consider the civic education embodied in the English National Curriculum as a case study.

Introduction: why education needs to concern itself with these issues. The role of the family and the school

Moral, personal and civic education are closely related areas but each raises distinct policy issues. One feature that they all share, however, is that they are thought to be practical subjects with a contested theoretical component. Another is that there is disagreement concerning whether or not they are most appropriately dealt with as a part of child-rearing in the home or as part of formal education within school. What are the relationships between these three areas? In this chapter we will address these questions.

Moral education concerns the relationship between right and wrong action and the abilities of children to distinguish the two and to engage in and support the former. Personal education concerns children's abilities to form their own personalities and to move towards self-realisation Civic education, on the other hand, is concerned with children's ability to understand and to take part in the political processes of their society. While it is difficult to see how one can have meaningful personal or civic education without moral education, it is undoubtedly possible to have moral education without either of the other two, at least in a formal sense. One might argue that this would lead to an incomplete education, but that is another issue. But it is also arguable that it is not the place of schooling to provide moral education either. We will examine the extent to which an accountable public education system should engage itself in these three areas, without at the same time producing prescriptions for each.

Moral, personal and civic education are all unavoidable aspects of education, even if they are not part of schooling. Education, as we saw, is a preparation for life and life unavoidably involves moral, personal and civic aspects. A schooling system's refusal to incorporate any one or all of them into the curriculum is an indication of the priorities of that schooling system, it is not and cannot be an elimination of them from the concept of education. Exclusion of them from schooling is due either to a judgement as to their *importance* (they are too unimportant for school to bother with), their *difficulty* (the subject matter is too inherently difficult or complex to be dealt with in school) or their *controversiality* (there is too much intra-communal and political disagreement about whether and how they should be taught). We shall examine the reasons for and against including some or all three in the school curriculum. It follows, then, that although moral, personal and civic education are necessarily aspects of education, they are not always given a role in *schooling*. This reflects the view that they are not part of the conception of education embraced by the school system.

Moral education: why we need it and what form it should take, including implicit moral education

Moral education in the sense introduced above is obviously indispensable to any preparation for life. Beyond this there is likely to be less agreement. Some maintain that the proper place for it is in the home (Holt 1984). Others maintain, on the contrary, that the state has a vital role in it. Others, like Hobbes, think that the state should at least have a stake in it (Hobbes 1968, Chapter 26). Undoubtedly one of the fears of those who think that it is a matter of parental responsibility is that allowing the state to have a role through the public education system will lead to state-sponsored morality, which will, in turn, diminish the power of individuals and civil society in relation to the state. Those who believe that parents should *not* have the main role in moral education believe that there is a danger that parentally conducted moral education will lead to adults who are unable to make their own choices about the kinds of lives that they wish to lead or, alternatively, who will be unable to respect certain categories of people, such as women, sufficiently.

The situation is complicated for liberals, who espouse a 'thin theory of the good'. This means that, in a liberal society made up of different interest groups there must be an attempt made to identify the shared values which enable such groups to live together in relative harmony. According to Rawls (1971, 1993), the kind of consensus that underpins a liberal society involves commitment to the greatest equal liberty, to fair equality of opportunity and to a weak distributive principle that ensures the position of the least well-off segment of society. Accordingly, moral views *consistent* with these positions are allowable. What they are will be the choice of particular communities, who will have different 'thick' or contentful conceptions of the good. However, moral positions that are *not consistent* with these principles of justice are not reasonable, that is, they do not form the basis for co-operation with other members of society, even if their own members consider them to underpin their own conceptions of what constitutes worthwhile lives. They serve no real function within the principles of a liberal polity and are, in a formal sense, unjust. This is not a trivial point: for example, rigid egalitarianism, which requires everyone to have exactly the same income and wealth might be said to be inconsistent with the greatest equal liberty principle; so also might a belief in discrimination between, say, girls and boys in respect of opportunities inconsistent with the fair equality of opportunity principle. So also is the libertarian belief that a charitable safety net is the only morally justifiable form of help for the poor; inconsistent with at least one interpretation of the principle that distributions should be to the greatest advantage of the least well-off.

Whatever we think of this view of liberalism, it poses problems for moral education, because it seems to suggest that much that now passes for moral education is not consistent with the principles of justice thus set out and should, therefore, be suppressed, whether it takes place at home or within school. It should be suppressed because to educate children in such a way would be to fail to prepare them to co-operate with other members of society for everyone's mutual advantage. Needless to say, many would be very uneasy with this. How could it be the case that a particular liberal view of morality should be allowed to suppress its rivals, even if they were sincerely considered to be right by those who held them? Liberalism of this kind seems, on the one hand, not to prescribe any particular range of what are worthwhile options and, at the same time, to forbid a whole range of beliefs being acted upon that seem to many to be essential to their own view of how their own children should be brought up. Something is wrong here.

In one sense, the 'thin theory of the good' is too thin, since it gives little or no indication of what range of options the society considers worthwhile. In another sense, it is too 'thick' since it *excludes* the content of many forms of moral education. In this sense, as Mulhall (1998) has argued, it is itself a substantive moral doctrine with its own moral commitments. As such, it is committed to certain views of what is or is not morally allowable. For example, Rawls' treatment of abortion suggests that forbidding termination of pregnancy in the first three months is unreasonable and may be cruel and oppressive (Rawls 1993, pp. 243–244, fn 32). Behind the denial of substantive moral content to liberal political doctrine, there lies a commitment to a doctrine that

includes a 'due respect for human life' and 'the equality of women as equal citizens' (ibid.). It is at least arguable that this is a substantive moral commitment
based on a particular, and controversial for some, interpretation of human
rights. The problem, as we see it, is that the liberal consensus on which civil
order is based should prescribe as little as possible regarding what is allowable. It
should not, however, shirk from saying something substantive about the range
of worthwhile options, if this is what a democratic majority want. Is this consistent? Groups who are willing to obey the laws laid down by democratically
elected majorities and who contribute to the upkeep of the society should be
allowed to bring up their children in ways that are consistent with those laws,
even if the government of the day has a particular view of what constitutes a
worthwhile life. According to this view, there is no one liberal policy on abortion which has to be applied in any society that can be called 'liberal'. Of
course, there has to be some policy, but its emergence will be a matter of political argument within the society.

If a government is unable to advance any substantive idea of the good, then
it is unclear to what extent the society thus governed is able to have a political
life that goes beyond suppressing views that fall outside its conception of what is
reasonable. Of course, there should be a consensus on which political life rests,
but this needs to encompass the minimum necessary for conflict to occur
through political rather than violent means. This entails a commitment to *tolerance* or the view that those who have views which are morally in conflict with
our own should have the right, within limits, to promote those views both
politically and within their own communities, provided they extend tolerance
to those who disagree with them. If liberal democracy implies anything, it
implies that all citizens have an equal right to consideration and justice, based
on a common individual interest in the maintenance of the conditions for a
worthwhile life, whatever that might be.

Tolerance does not imply that one *likes* the views and practices that one tol-
erates, if that were so, one would not need to tolerate them. Tolerance implies
that one continues to co-operate with people whose views one dislikes and even
despises. Why should people do this? The reason is that to work out differences
amicably rather than through coercion is in everyone's long-term interests,
since groups that are currently in the majority may well not be so in the future.
What are these limits of tolerance? They are much weaker than the bounds of
reasonableness suggested by Rawls (1993), which imply that only co-operation
that *benefits* all constitutes the basis for satisfactory civil and political life. They
will include: (1) a principle of justice that makes all equal before the law and
entitled to fair treatment (Gray 1995); (2) a legal ban on violence against
persons and property and expropriation of personal property (personal property
being the holdings that are the minimum necessary to live an independent life);
and (3) the allowing of a plurality of moral, political and religious views, subject
to the limits of (1) and (2) above. This implies that individuals and communities will be willing to co-operate even if they suffer specific *losses* in doing so

which fall short of violations of (1), (2) and (3) above. They will be willing to do so because civil peace is nearly always preferable to civil war.

Of course, none of this would work without a liberal consensus. But that is also the case with the stronger form of overlapping consensus that Rawls advocates. Both require the habit of living together in a form of co-operative endeavour which ultimately depends on ingrained atttitudes and habits of tolerance and compromise. No kind of liberalism can be imposed by formal agreement if the relevant habits to adhere to it do not yet exist (Hume 1978, BK III, Part II, Section V). But the kind of consensus that we suggest is far easier to achieve than the one advocated by Rawls and has none of its disadvantage of not allowing most of what we would call political and civil life. It is easier to achieve because it demands less and is more compatible with a range of achievable liberal and even non-liberal states than the consensus advocated by Rawls. He can find no example of his version of political liberalism, not even the United States, which seems to be the society which comes nearest to the principles enshrined in political liberalism as he sees it.

Given these considerations, it is possible to see that a liberal political society should allow diverse forms of moral education subject to the constraints above. Nearly all moral traditions find little difficulty in agreeing with respect for life, limb and personal property (points (1) and (2) above). Some, but by no means all, have difficulty with (3), the principle of tolerance. But liberalism on our view is not just a set of principles, but a set of attitudes and dispositions that inclines us to tolerance. One condition of value diversity and tolerance within a liberal society is that all groups share such attitudes and dispositions. It is important to realise that this does not mean that they give up their own views, merely that they accept that there may be limitations to the extent that they can be implemented (Gray 1995, Chapter 5; Winch 1996, Chapter 3).

That said, moral education at home and school should be consistent and, provided principles 1–3 are adhered to, there should be enough in common between the public education system and child-rearing in the home and community to avoid conflict. At the same time, the divergent religious and moral views that different parents may have can be developed within communities. We can thus see that a diversity of moral education could exist within an atmosphere of mutual tolerance. 'But', many liberals would say, 'a problem still remains'. 'We could imagine children growing up tolerant but completely blinkered when it comes to considering the point of view of other people. They might tolerate other views because they have been habituated to do so, but be incapable of having any imaginative sympathy whatsoever for these views.' This would, in our opinion, be a crippling constraint on the requirement of tolerance. Tolerance would become mechanical, divorced from either sympathy or understanding and therefore unlikely to last. Unless one can have some imaginative insight into, and therefore some sympathy for, views alien to one's own, the ability to negotiate and to compromise, which are the natural outcomes of a tolerant outlook, will be difficult to achieve.

Our position leaves it open at the moment as to whether or not there should be distinct schools catering to distinct moral and religious traditions. We will take a closer look at these issues in Chapter 10, but for the moment we will point out that the constraints that we have sketched out are compatible with a number of different ways of dealing with cultural and value diversity in the context of a public education system sponsored by a liberal plural society.

Critical rationality as a requirement of school-based moral education

How then, can condition (3), concerning tolerance and compromise, be met in a way that is going to work in the long term? We maintain that this condition implies that the development of critical rationality, while desirable in relation to various aspects of the curriculum (see Chapters 2, 3 and 10), is also of great relevance to moral education. Critical rationality is required to provide the necessary insight into the possible weaknesses in one's own beliefs to a degree that one can at least appreciate that there are alternative points of view that are not necessarily wicked. This allows people to take seriously the idea that sincere, well-meaning people may nevertheless hold views that one believes to be profoundly mistaken. Critical rationality, however, enables more than this. In seeing what the weaknesses of one's own views are, one is also in a better position to assess what are the strongest and most valuable aspects of those beliefs, as well as those features of one's own beliefs that one would be most reluctant to give up the implementation of in the world. This awareness is itself a prerequisite for attempts to establish compromises about the implementation of beliefs and value systems in the world.

The content of moral education

We can now briefly consider the content of moral education. A liberal society would expect its citizens to uphold the right to life, personal property and basic standards of fairness to all citizens. It would also expect them to be able to adopt a critically rational stance towards their own and others' moral beliefs. Beyond this, however, we are disinclined to prescribe either a general approach to moral education, or the philosophy underlying that approach. This means that moral education can be based either on the development of character or on the development of adherence to rules of conduct (Carr and Steutel 1999; Haydon 1999). It can either be concerned with the consequences of actions or with the value of the actions themselves. It will, however, contain, in some degree or other, elements of the following:

1 Moral education as practical preparation for life.
2 Moral education as knowledge of right and wrong.
3 Moral education as knowledge of what people believe to be right or wrong.

Point 1 concerns the development of the ability to conduct oneself and to form moral judgements in the everyday contexts of life, as well as in more particular situations, such as friendships, sexual relationships, the family and the workplace. There are different conceptions of how this should be done. One, deriving from the work of Aristotle, suggests that it be best achieved through the development of character traits which allow fine-grained, but essentially personal judgements to be made that are appropriate to the situation in hand (Aristotle 1925; Carr 1991, Carr and Steutel 1999). Another, utilitarian in inspiration (that is, concerned with the maximisation of pleasure or preference satisfaction), emphasises the ability to make correct judgements about the *consequences* of action (Mill 1861; Scarre 1997). Yet another tradition emphasises the ability to recognise and to follow moral rules (Kant 1948; Haydon 1999). The first of these traditions pays particular attention to the practical side of preparation, but, we would argue, in such a way that morally educated persons will pay due regard to whatever principles of right and wrong conduct obtain in their society. The second places particular emphasis on point 1 and in particular on being able to work out consequences that lead to preference-satisfaction for as many people as possible. The third lays particular emphasis on point 2, and thus on development of the recognition of and ability to follow moral rules. But utilitarian tradition does not dismiss the importance of rule-guidedness completely (see Smart 1973), nor does the rule-based tradition completely ignore the importance of character development as a means of developing the ability to recognise the binding nature of moral rules. Different moral traditions will place different emphases on points 1 and 2.

Criterion 3 is not particularly important in normative moral education, that is, moral education that prepares one to behave morally and to evaluate the actions of others. From our point of view, however, normative moral education is not sufficient for preparation for life in a liberal society. We have noted the fact of *value pluralism*, that different groups within a society have different values and we have also noted that liberalism, as a working political system, requires the ability to tolerate, to understand and to arrive at compromises over the implementation of different values. This requires that those alternatives be understood, hence the importance of point 3. We are not claiming that 3 has any priority over normative moral education. Indeed, our view is that one has to have a secure basis of moral preparation before one can be in a position to consider moral alternatives. Why is this? Briefly, one needs an understanding of morality and why it is important *in a practical sense* before one can consider alternatives. It is part of the normative nature of morality that one recognises its demands, whether they be in terms of consideration of consequences, appropriate judgement or the recognition of binding rules. One is considering alternative normative moral systems, alternative ways in which moral demands are made on one. In order to consider and evaluate such alternatives, one needs some understanding of what a moral demand is and why it is important. We suggest that knowledge of moral alternatives in one's native moral tradition is a vital part of a complete moral education, not necessarily appropriate to its early stages (see also Winch 1998, Chapter 14).

Personal education

As we have already seen, morality concerns our conduct, our relationship with others and our evaluation of our conduct and that of others. Necessarily, much action in a civilised society is *other-regarding*, that is, it is concerned with the consequences of our actions for other people. Most forms of normative moral education place a great deal of emphasis on the importance of other-regarding considerations for moral behaviour. Some even deny the importance of any-thing much beyond this (see Schopenhauer 1883). It is, however, a characteris-tic feature of liberal societies that, in some sense, self-fulfilment is seen as an essential constituent of a worthwhile life. Liberalism has even been accused of emphasising self-fulfilment to such a degree that it ignores the need to pay due regard to the interests of others (Phillips 1996, Chapter 8). There are varieties of liberalism that might be open to this accusation however, we do not think it is an essential feature of liberal thought. We do not, however, think that it is an essential feature of liberal thought. It is true, however, that liberalism places a significant emphasis on personal fulfilment and hence on what are sometimes called *self-regarding* considerations.

While most liberals believe that self-regarding considerations should not come before concern for others, it is important for liberal education that young people learn how to lead lives that are fulfilling for themselves, and this is bound to involve self-regarding considerations even if, ultimately, leading a worthwhile life is bound up with being connected with larger social projects (White 1995). Children and young people need to know the following at least: how to conduct themselves so as to maintain self-respect and the respect of others; how to express their own wishes and negotiate their fulfilment; how to understand what they are truly interested in and capable of; how to persevere to achieve personal goals. These abilities are all vital if young people are going to live successfully in the context of their families, school, peer groups, friend-ship groups and in the formation and maintenance of sentimental and sexual relationships. They clearly have an other-regarding moral dimension, but they also have an inescapable personal dimension in the sense that other people are indispensable to the achievement of one's personal projects, and also in the sense that one needs to have some sense of who one is before one can embark on one's own projects. Such is the domain of personal education.

The content of personal education

In Chapter 7, we will consider the liberal claim that education is largely a preparation for self-determination, or the ability to choose and pursue a desir-able choice of a way of life for oneself. This is essentially a self-regarding aim, and, as such, implicit in much of personal education. However, there are more specific things to be said about personal education. Of particular importance is the ability to get on with other people. Children who are unable to do this are unlikely to be able to pursue their own projects, since the great majority of these depend for their realisation on the co-operation of others. This does not mean that one merely falls in with the wishes of others, but that one co-operates while maintaining one's own integrity. The second point concerns self-knowledge and self-mastery. One cannot form plans for one's life if one does not know what one is interested in, what one's abilities are and one does not have any capacity for persistence in one's projects. These seem to constitute the basic features of personal education. How should they be taught? Much of the education in getting on with others involves family life and, later, school life and friendship and peer groups. One becomes good at this sort of thing by doing it. However, for various reasons, e.g. persistent selfishness, tactlessness, the dislike of their peers, we know that many fail.

Personal education, then, seems to involve an element of advice or, as it is nowadays called, *counselling*. No teacher can turn a socially inept youngster into the most popular child in the playground merely by dispensing advice, but advice based on wide knowledge and experience can help to avert future social disaster and provide the basis for a more viable social life in the longer term. Nor should the practice of *simulation* be excluded, in which potentially tricky social situations are set up and possible ways of negotiating one's way through them examined. Third, what is known as *vicarious* experience may also be valuable, in which, for example, through literature or drama, young people can see that the problems they face are not uniquely theirs and that there are ways of avoiding disaster through wise decision-making. We do not take a view as to whether or not personal education should have an explicit place on the curriculum as a separate subject. We do suggest, however, that it is difficult to provide a full personal education completely within the family, as there are not enough situations available there that one is likely to meet in life. This suggests that school, or something like it, for example, clubs or associations, are going to be a necessary vehicle of a full personal education.

Civic education

Civic education concerns the preparation of young people for their future roles as citizens. This concerns their roles in the political and communal lives of their societies, at whatever level they participate. It would normally be an expectation that the citizens of a democratic society be able to vote in elections and to understand, at some level, the issues that they are being asked to vote upon. Typically, in a society like ours, these institutions will range from the local (local authorities) to the national (national and federal parliaments) to the regional (EU bodies). At each level there are different issues, but at the same time common features. Most people will not wish to stand for elected office within the political structures of the society, even at the most humble munici-pal level. We may reasonably expect them though, to appreciate the issues that they are electing members to represent them on. Not only that, but we would expect them to have some reasonable appreciation of the decision-making powers which these different bodies have and the division of power between them. It makes a substantial difference to know, for example, that the Scottish Parliament, like the UK one, has powers over the raising of taxes, but unlike the UK Parliament, no powers to conduct foreign policy. Likewise, it is relevant for an elector to the Welsh Assembly to realise that the Assembly enjoys neither of these powers. Similar points apply to citizens of the USA. They need to know what powers municipal and county authorities, the states and the Federal Government share among themselves before they can meaningfully participate in democratic politics. All of this constitutes a 'weak' or minimal conception of citizenship. Stronger conceptions of citizenship would involve increasing levels of participation in civil society and political institutions. There are questions first about whether such higher levels of participation are possible or even desirable in a liberal democracy and, second, concerning whether it is possible to educate all young people towards such stronger forms of citizenship.

Let us look more closely at what is expected of individuals as citizens in terms of knowledge, skill and understanding. Knowledge of the political struc-tures of one's polity is a prerequisite of participation. This knowledge does not have to be extremely detailed, but must be sufficient to appreciate, in broad terms, how the powers of different bodies at different levels of the polity relate to each other. Naturally, those who wish to take an active part by standing for elected office will need to know quite a lot more. However, it is not enough to know some facts, one must also be able to appreciate what it is like to stand for office, to weigh up arguments, to vote and to form policy. It is worth noting in this context that in many societies citizens are nominated by lottery to serve as jurors on serious cases which involve the well-being and future freedom of their fellow citizens, quite apart from any other roles which they may care to take on a voluntary basis.

A consequence of this is that future citizens have to develop certain *skills* as well as acquire a certain amount of *knowledge*. The best way to do this is to provide practical contexts in which these skills can be developed by learning to exercise them. But it would be a mistake to see civic education solely in terms of skill and knowledge. An important aspect of it is to do with attitudes and understanding. This brings up an important and often misunderstood point about the nature of skills. If we confine ourselves to examples such as typing, counting or the sawing of wood, then the skill itself does not appear to have any moral implications. Naturally one needs certain virtues to do these things, like patience and attention to detail, but the skill itself is largely describable in terms of fine or gross motor dexterity or mental agility. On the other hand, 'skills' such as the ability to see someone else's point of view, or to argue one's case in a reasonable way, to restrain oneself in the presence of views that one finds repugnant or to compromise over the implementation of values that one holds dearly seem to be of a different order.

'Skill' may be the wrong term, 'ability' may be better, if it avoids the implication that what is involved is in any way simple (see Chapter 3). These abilities involve reaction to other people in situations of considerable moral significance and, to this extent, presuppose a considerable degree of what we have called 'moral, personal and social education'. They cannot be taught except through some form of practical engagement with situations where these abilities are relevant and, perhaps, a certain degree of vicarious experience. So, for instance, schools and colleges provide opportunities for some kinds of elective autonomous bodies which are able to provide all their students with the power to carry out some self-directed functions. But also, because such practical engagement must necessarily be limited, students need a certain degree of vicarious experience which enables them to identify with the views of others, which may be nurtured by engagement with literature.

There are three possible objections to this proposal. The first is a philosophical one, that citizenship is not a proper concern of education. The second is political, that civic education will become a form of indoctrination. The third is practical, that there is insufficient room on a crowded curriculum for civic education. The first objection we believe to be wrong. The other two have some substance, however, and need to be taken seriously whatever one's final view of the role of civic education.

The first objection is wrong from the point of view that we adopt, that education is preparation for life. Becoming a citizen is an unavoidable aspect of life. Therefore, civic education is a central part of education. While this argument is valid, it does not, of itself, show that civic education should take place in school. It might, for example, be adequately dealt with in the home and in organisations in civil society such as churches, clubs and other voluntary organisations. We need to know what the reasons are for making civic education part of the school curriculum. Here the argument becomes practical: the claim would be that school is the most suitable place in which to carry out civic education. Other institutions are either unable to do it properly or children might fail to belong to organisations that could manage it. Very few children in the UK, for example, now attend churches. Furthermore, assigning civic education to voluntary organisations leaves one vulnerable to the second objection, that civic education is in danger of becoming a form of indoctrination. If one left civic education to political parties or churches, for example, the danger – as with the curriculum as such (see Chapter 2) – would be especially acute. Schools, it could be argued, because they involve all children before a certain age and because they are themselves ultimately under democratic control, are ideally placed to carry out this role.

What of the third objection, that there is insufficient room on a crowded curriculum for civic education? We might be convinced of the theoretical value of civic education, dubious that it could be provided by the family or civil society, and yet unconvinced that there is a place for it on the school curriculum. Interestingly, we don't say this about moral education as it is impossible to be educated without learning about the importance of one's dealings with other people. Nevertheless, moral education does not always have an established place on the school curriculum, but finds its way into education through extra-curricular activities. Shouldn't this also be the case for civic education? To some extent this is true. If some form of consultative and governing structures in which students have a role to play is incorporated into the governance of schools, then there is an opportunity for the practical abilities, together with attitudes such as inclination to compromise and to tolerance that civic education should develop, to be practised.

Some of the problems that confront citizens receive a very rich and sympathetic treatment in literature. For example, in English literature, Disraeli's novel *Sybil* provides material for thought about the dilemmas involved in being a citizen and fighting for social justice; Kipling's neglected *Stalky and Co.* provides a subtle account of the methods used by the nineteenth-century public school system to promote an enthusiastic but, in some limited respects, independent-minded imperial elite; the dilemmas faced by citizens fighting in wars in which they no longer believe are movingly dealt with in Sassoon's *Memoirs of an Infantry Officer*. Moving further afield, writers such as Alfred Andersch (in *Zanzibar*) and Joseph Roth (in *Radetskymarch*), Henrik Ibsen (in *An Enemy of the People*) and Joseph Heller (in *Catch 22*) have all discussed the difficulties of reconciling personal with political or patriotic commitments. Real-life examples, in the form of historical case studies, are also highly instructive.

The factual side of civic education can partly be covered in history and geography. The growth of institutions and the basic divisions of politics and allocations of resources in the world can be dealt with in these subjects, but this, of itself, is unlikely to be sufficient. In order to function in a modern democracy, citizens need to know what the political institutions of their society are and how they work. This is knowledge that will not normally be fully acquired through osmosis, but requires a degree of direct instruction. There is, therefore, an irreducible element of specific subject matter in civic education that cannot be dealt with elsewhere. Given that there is such an irreducible minimum, there is then a question as to whether, given that some civic education should appear on the curriculum, the elements of skill development and understanding should not also appear.

Contemporary civic education in England and Wales: a case study

As we have seen, England has had a national curriculum only since 1988, explicit aims of education since 1999 and nationally prescribed civic education since 2002 (McLaughlin 2000). While in the earlier years of education, civic education is closely tied to personal aspects of education, it becomes a distinct strand in the secondary curriculum from the ages of 11 to 16 (DfEE 1999). Previous to that, it could be said that insofar as civic education was recognised as an aspect of education, it was taught implicitly. The National Curriculum aims, set out in 1999, clearly set out preparation for citizenship as an aspect of those aims. Moral, personal and civic education all receive specific mention: moral education should 'develop principles for distinguishing between right and wrong', personal education 'should promote pupils' self-esteem and emotional well-being and help them to form worthwhile and satisfying relationships', while civic education should

> help them to be responsible and caring citizens capable of contributing to the development of a just society. It should promote equal opportunities and enable pupils to challenge discrimination and stereotyping. It should develop their awareness and understanding of, and respect for, the environments in which they live, and secure their commitment to sustainable development at a personal, local, national and global level. It should also equip pupils as consumers to make informed judgements and independent decisions and to understand their responsibilities and rights.
>
> (All quotes DfEE 1999, p. 11)

One thus moves from aspirations of great generality in the case of moral education, to more explicit ones for personal education to quite explicit ones in the case of civic education. In the light of the discussion above, this should not be surprising. As a liberal democracy, the UK is wary of laying down moral principles too explicitly, for fear of excluding those of some groups. As a liberal society committed to individual autonomy and independence (see Chapter 7), it is not surprising that personal education aims to allow them to develop the personal attributes necessary for this (whether these are sufficient rather than necessary is another matter), while civic education refers to a contribution, to justice, meritocratic values, environmental responsibility and consumerism. While explicit, it is also the case that the civic values enshrined here are relatively uncontroversial and also susceptible of a range of interpretations. Arriving at a satisfactory notion of equal opportunities is, for example, notoriously difficult (Barry 1995).

The Crick Report (QCA 1988) advocates active citizenship and as well as essential knowledge, skills, values, attitudes, dispositions and understanding (Section 3.1). Active citizens in this sense, are those who do more than understand their institutions and contemporary political issues and vote, they are individuals who run for office and organise political movements and events, not to mention taking a prominent role in the institutions of civil society. The Crick Report is also mindful of the danger of indoctrination referred to above and, instead of prescribing content strongly, instead sets out tightly defined learning outcomes, which can be achieved through a variety of routes (Section

6.10.1). It may be, however, that the aspiration to active citizenship is an ideal which may be realised for a few, but not for all. Certainly, the aims of the school curriculum do not prescribe anything that looks like active citizenship and this for a good reason. It is not going to be the case that most citizens are going to be active ones in the sense above.

Conclusion

Moral, personal and civic education are all indispensable components of a complete education in a liberal democracy. This is recognised in the contemporary English school curriculum. Modern liberal democratic societies contain citizens and communities with a variety of beliefs, often incompatible in some respects with each other. We saw that universalist liberalism of the kind advocated by Rawls is both too prescriptive (it excludes options that one might expect to see in some liberal societies) and too unprescriptive (it has nothing positive to say about what might constitute worthwhile ways of living a life). Liberal societies should be able to indicate to their citizens what are considered to be worthwhile options and, being liberal societies, we would expect them to leave a wide variety of options open. Moral education should not only enable young people to recognise and strive for what is worthwhile but to appreciate that there are other points of view than one's own, which are also worthy of respect and taking seriously.

The fact that people have choices about how they want to live their lives and are responsible for those choices means that they need the personal qualities to realise a worthwhile life. Crucially this involves being able to co-operate with and to secure the co-operation of others in various dimensions of life. This is the rationale for some form of personal education. Lives have a public as well as a private dimension. In liberal democratic society adults are expected to play a role, however small, in the political governance of their society and in the institutions of civil society. For this reason, some form of civic education is an indispensable part of education.

Questions for further discussion

1 Should schools have a role in moral education?
2 Is it sufficient to teach children the rules of right conduct in order to morally educate them?
3 Should sex education be about relationships as well as biology?
4 Can we teach young people how to be popular?
5 How practical should citizenship education be? Give examples.
6 What is an active citizen? Can schools develop them?

Further reading

Moral education is currently a lively and disputed field. There are both polemical and more serious works on the topic. On the polemical side, see, for example, Melanie Phillips' *All Must Have Prizes* (London, Little and Brown, 1996). A thoughtful defence of a rule-based moral education can be found in Graham Haydon's *Values, Virtues and Violence* (Oxford, Blackwell, 1999). A distinguished collection of articles on virtue-based approaches is provided by David Carr and Jan Steutel (eds), *Virtue Ethics and Moral Education* (London, Routledge, 1999). Less has been written on social education, but again, Phillips provides a lively treatment of some of the issues in Chapter 13. David Archard's *Sex Education* (London, PESGB, 2000) provides a good introduction to a specific topic in personal education, while John White's *Education and Personal Well-being in a Secular Universe* (London, Institute of Education, 1995) provides a broad survey of the topic. The same author's *Education and the Good Life* (London, Routledge, 1990) provides more detailed treatment of some of these topics.

Stephen Mulhall provides a detailed critique of the relationship between liberalism and civic education in 'Political Liberalism and Civic Education', *Journal of Philosophy of Education*, 32, 3: 161–176 (1998). Detailed discussion of issues connected with the UK can be found in T.H. McLaughlin's 'Citizenship Education in England: The Crick Report and Beyond', *Journal of Philosophy of Education*, 34, 4: 541–570 (2000) and Bernard Crick's 'The Presuppositions of Citizenship Education', *Journal of Philosophy of Education* (1999). For a critical look at the Crick Report, see A. Flew, *Education for Citizenship* (London, Institute of Economic Affairs, 2000).

Chapter 7

Autonomy and liberal education

This chapter opens by considering the nature of modern liberal education and the significance of the educational aim of individual autonomy in such a society. It then goes on to look at what autonomy involves, contrasting it with independence. It is argued that the capacity for autonomy is a complex one and needs to be developed educationally if it is to be properly acquired. We then go on to examine the contrast between weak and strong autonomy and argue that, although most liberal societies sanction strong autonomy, it is difficult to see how schools could do other than promote the capacity for weak autonomy in their pupils. The educational implications of autonomy are then drawn out so that we can see what an autonomous person would have to be able to do, in order to be autonomous. Finally, we look at the place of education for autonomy in a liberal society and briefly consider the policy implications of educating for autonomy.

Conservative and modern liberal education

Throughout this book we examine various aspects of a liberal conception of education which is concerned with preparing individuals to lead their own lives. *Conservative* liberal education in the past emphasised the importance of acquaintance with the dominant culture of the society and with the acquisition of character traits such as self-control and independence in order to do so. We present a modern version of this in our treatment of culture and the curriculum. However, whereas the traditional form of conservative liberal education was designed for those destined for particular positions in society and also maintained many of the features of the way of life of the gentry, our version is designed for all those being educated.

One of the features of a *modern* version of liberal education, however, is its concern with the ability to prepare oneself for life within a society in which values, beliefs and social roles are fluid and where there are few, if any, occupations which are so stable that one can predict with confidence what one's place in society is going to be. The emphasis is on preparation for choice of value, belief and occupation within the context of social fluidity. Modern liberalism emphasises the ability to cope in such circumstances in a way that allows for individuals to make considered choices without at the same time allowing the amount of choice to lead to a paralysis in decision-making. *Radical* liberal educators emphasise the role of education in preparing young people to make choices that potentially challenge the values and beliefs of the society in which they are going to live. Foremost among the liberal educators in this tradition was Rousseau ([1762], 1910), who believed that the role of education was itself to prepare society for radical transformation. Rousseau's radicalism has strict limits however, as can be seen in his treatment of relations between the sexes (ibid., Book V). In practice, there is a great deal of common ground between modern and radical liberal educators. Indeed, it would be true to say that some exponents of modern liberal education have taken over one of the central aims of the radical conception, namely, its commitment to challenge the existing order. This leads to problems for the modern liberal conception which we will examine below.

The modern interpretation of liberal education

The central goal of the modern liberal conception of education is that of individual preparation for *autonomy*. Someone who is *autonomous* is able to make choices about how they are to live and the values they are going to adopt. To be autonomous is not just to be free to choose *how* one is going to achieve one's ends in life, it is to possess the freedom to choose the ends themselves. Why is autonomy thought to be so important by modern liberal educators? The main reason is to be found in the nature of contemporary society. Modern liberal democratic societies have the following central features. They allow for the freedom of movement, of way of life and of belief. Market forces, which dominate the economic, political and social life of such societies, are constantly refashioning institutions like the family, the business and even religious beliefs. There are very few familiar institutions that we can expect to remain unchanged within our lifetimes. Given the rapid economic changes that the market promotes, it is also unlikely that we can expect to remain in the same job or even the same kind of job over the course of a lifetime. A democratic form of government means that people have choices over their governments and also to some extent over the values that their society expresses.

In these circumstances it is thought by many that individual autonomy is the only feasible educational goal. The only feature of our lives that will remain unchanged is constant change. We can cope with this only if we are able to select, from the bewildering range of alternatives open to us, those that most suit our interests and talents. We need also to be able to reflect on, and if necessary to revise, our life goals if we are to keep up with rapid change. Crucially, some think that this means that we must have the option of making choices that society would not currently think are worthwhile. If no value or opportunity is set in stone, we cannot ask people to make choices as if their available alternatives were permanent. Even if individual autonomy were not a goal for every society, it is difficult, on this argument, to fail to see that autonomy is a necessity for a worthwhile life in our kind of society. It cannot then be enough for education to prepare people for *independence* if all that this means is that they are free to choose means to attain ends that others have chosen for them.

Suppose a certain society were to determine that women should marry. Given that they had to marry, but that they had the choice of which man to marry, such a society would allow women a degree of independence. They would not be *autonomous* because they would not be able to make a meaningful life-choice of whether or not to marry. When women are allowed to decide whether or not to marry, then they are not just independent with respect to marriage, but autonomous with respect to it. A woman who has her marriage partner chosen for her irrespective of whether or not she wishes to marry is not even independent.

The goal of autonomy and non-traditional democratic societies

According to this way of looking at things, it is a necessary feature of a worthwhile life in a liberal democratic market-oriented society that people are autonomous. Since the capacity for autonomous choice does not just happen, but has to be cultivated, one of the central functions of education is to prepare young people to be autonomous. This does not entail that only being autonomous makes lives worthwhile. Given that autonomy is a necessary condition of a worthwhile life in *our* society, it does not follow that it is a necessary condition for a worthwhile life in *any* society. To pursue our example, a woman who did not have a choice about whether or not to marry, but who could marry whom she chose could still have a worthwhile life. It is also arguable that some forms of non-independent life can be worthwhile. Some might dispute this. It might be argued that there are universal features of what makes human life worthwhile, which do not vary from culture to culture. Among these central features is that of self-determination of one's ends in life. It would follow that preparation for a life that was not autonomous would not be a worthwhile education, since it could not be a preparation for a worthwhile life. We do not accept this claim. However, we do think that autonomy is a necessary condition of a worthwhile life in the kind of society that we have described. At the same time, however, it must be recognised that some people do not wish to be autonomous. In order to give them a sense of what worthwhile choices are available to them, they need to be able to make the choice not to be autonomous in an autonomous way, that is, conscious of the alternatives that are available.

Liberal universalists hold that liberal values, including autonomy, hold good in all places under all circumstances. But one does not have to believe this in order to hold that autonomy is a necessary condition for living a worthwhile life in democratic market-oriented societies. Liberal universalism is sometimes defended by the device of asking what anyone who was not acquainted with their particular circumstances would choose as the ground rules for a society in which they could construct a worthwhile life for themselves (see for example, Rawls 1993, Lecture VIII). In such circumstances it would be rational to choose a society in which one was autonomous, since other arrangements might force upon one ways of life that were uncongenial. However, it does not follow from the fact, even if it were true, that under these circumstances one would choose an autonomous life, that the only kind of worthwhile life in any circumstances is an autonomous one. It does not seem to us, therefore, that the value of autonomy as an educational aim has universal significance. It does, however, have enormous importance in liberal market democracies.

The conceptions of right and the good: versions of liberalism

Universalist liberalism of the kind described above suggests that a rational person ignorant of their actual situation in life would choose the conditions for autonomy, together with some other conditions such as equality of opportunity and a certain level of resources (ibid.). Beyond this, however, there would be no requirements on a just liberal state to prescribe the elements of a worthwhile life. Under these conditions of choice we would have no knowledge concerning our abilities, tastes or community values. What is more, we could be reasonably certain that other members of our society would have conceptions of a worthwhile life that differed from our own. We would not, therefore, choose to live in a society that prescribed to others how they should live, since this would not be rational, leaving our own values open to suppression. On this view, all that the state can do is set up the conditions for justice and leave the development of conceptions of what is and what is not a worthwhile life to individuals and communities.

It seems to follow from this that an education system funded by and accountable to the state should have no business in prescribing to young people the choices that are available to them. This seems to follow because it is no part of the business of the state to recommend any particular way of living a life so long as it conforms to the conditions of justice. At first sight it might appear as if this leaves almost no role to the education system, but this is not actually the case. The education system still needs to equip young people with the knowledge and skill to make their own life choices. The knowledge and skill that they require to make their own life choices are very extensive. Schools and colleges still have an enormous task in developing autonomy even without promoting particular forms of worthwhile life. The problem is not so much that a state education system has no role in these circumstances, but rather that it has a role that cannot be fulfilled. It cannot prepare children to be autonomous adults and at the same time prepare them to make choices that are not worthwhile. We saw in Chapter 6 that liberal civic education requires that they be brought up to evaluate as adults what should and should not be seen as worthwhile by their society. This is a very different task from that of promoting some non-worthwhile choices as options. While it may be possible to envisage a society run on such lines, so that no particular conception of the good is promoted by the state (although some, like Gray 1995, dispute this), it is much more difficult to envisage an education system run in this way, for reasons that we will explore below.

The central features of autonomy

First, however, we need to look more closely at the main elements involved in being autonomous. The first, that we have already considered, is the ability to choose the kind of life that one wishes to lead, or, to put it another way, one's ends in life. These may consist of vocational choices but also such matters as the kind of religion or ethical system that one wishes to adopt. Some writers, like Callan (1993), stress the importance of *self-mastery* or the ability to adhere to one's projects in the face of temptations, doubts and difficulties, as the key feature of the concept. Our view is that self-mastery is important for autonomy, but as a condition for making and carrying through life-choices. One can possess self-mastery and not be autonomous, for example, if one is a slave and wishes to make the best of one's condition. However, it is difficult to see how someone could be autonomous without at the same time having a degree of self-mastery. One would be at the mercy of circumstances, moods and the opinions of others that would threaten to disrupt one's freely chosen projects.

To say that someone is capable of making as important a choice as the kind of life that one is going to lead, and then carrying that choice through, is to imply at the same time that one has the necessary degree of self-mastery to do so. So self-mastery is an essential attribute of autonomy. There are further important conditions. First, it is necessary that one be both rational and informed enough to do so. To be rational in this sense is to be capable of evaluating choices in terms of one's preferences, abilities, personal knowledge and knowledge of the options available in the society in which one lives. Most commentators are not happy with the idea that an autonomous person could be someone who makes vital choices on impulse without considering their possible consequences, or someone who changes their mind from one short period of time to another. Given this consensus, it is important to see what the rationality condition for autonomous choice amounts to and what its consequences for someone's education are. We have more to say about this below. This brings us straight to another point. Being autonomous is something that one *achieves*, if one achieves it at all, at a certain stage of maturity, not before adolescence at the earliest. Autonomy concerns decisions that one has to make concerning the future direction of one's adult life and cannot be based on a childish view of the world in which the capacity for decision-making about the future course of one's life is not yet fully formed.

The next thing to say concerns *preferences*. The preferences that one needs to take into account are those that are long-lasting and considered. The whims and impulses of childhood, or even of one's more frivolous adult moments, are not suitable bases for autonomous decision-making. The reason is that one needs to be confident that one's preferences will sustain one through a life choice, that they will not let one down by disappearing and leaving one with a course of life that seems to be futile and unrewarding. Deep-rooted and long-lasting preferences normally issue from mature reflection about the possibilities open to one in the light of reasonable self-knowledge about one's values, interests and abilities. It is natural to think that education has a very important role in the formation of preferences, not least through the development of self-knowledge. But the role of education goes deeper than this, since one can only have self-knowledge if there is something about oneself that is worth knowing. In other words, one has to have values, interests and abilities. These do not emerge from nowhere, but need to be cultivated through educational processes.

At the very least, this entails, in terms of values, that one is presented with a range of potentially worthwhile principles by which to live one's life. These could include: a belief in fairness and justice, a consideration for one's physical and social environment and a commitment to the value of some forms of collective action. One might reply that no liberal should privilege one set of values above any others. Should we present children with the apparently unpleasant principles of egotism and the denial of the value of collective action as one possible set of values which they might adopt as a life plan? We will reserve judgement on this question for the moment, and confine ourselves to the observation that it is not an absurd question for liberals, who hold that the choice of values is important in the formation of autonomous people. The more restricted one's value choices are, the more difficult it is to be genuinely autonomous, it might be said. The question of formation of interests and abilities is probably more straightforward. Once we exclude whims, we can assume that the interests that will form the basis of a life plan are reasonable, well grounded and stable. Once again, we need to present children with a range of potential interests that will allow them to develop some that are well grounded and stable. However, they cannot do this unless they also acquire knowledge and skill. For example, children who wonder whether or not their interests fall within the strictly academic or the more practical sides of life need to be exposed to both in order to make a meaningful choice about either.

We need, then, to provide either within or outside school, a suitable range of possibilities, which include practical possibilities. It is true that some of these can be developed outside school, just as some academic possibilities can. However, not to introduce any in a systematic and carefully structured way is to risk depriving large numbers of children, possibly the majority, of the opportunities that academically-minded children have to experience potential academic interests in a systematic and carefully structured way. The development of autonomy seems, then, to require a broad curriculum in which values and both academic and more practical subjects are introduced in such a way that children can engage with them in a sufficiently meaningful way to get the self-knowledge necessary for a considered autonomous choice.

One final point is worth mentioning about the requirements for autonomy. Most commentators agree that an autonomous choice ought to be rational. In this context this means that, given one's values, abilities and self-knowledge, one makes a choice that best matches these attributes. One has, therefore to be able to conduct reasoning of the form: 'given what I know about what I value, what I enjoy and what I am good at, and given that I also know what are the possibilities available to me in my society and the relative likelihood of my realising these possibilities, I will choose from among the following available possibilities the ones that best suit what I know about myself.' Whether one believes that such rationality can be developed independently of the acquisition of skill and subject knowledge or that it has to be developed within established curriculum subjects, it is evident that one needs such a capacity if one is to make an informed choice. The curriculum does, therefore, in order to develop the capacity for autonomous decision-making, have to develop *rationality* as well as knowledge and practical skill.

Independence, weak and strong autonomy

Having seen what is involved in autonomy in general, it is now time to concentrate on different kinds of autonomy and to seek to determine what kind we should expect a state education system to develop. As we saw, someone is *independent* if they are able to choose means to ends that have been determined beforehand. To use our previous example, a young woman is independent with respect to marriage if she is able to choose a marriage partner. She would not be independent with respect to marriage if her husband were to be chosen for her. In a society which sanctions this, we might suppose, marriage would be seen as the only worthwhile life for a young woman. It is worth pointing out that in many societies people are independent, rather than autonomous, and many people in many societies are not independent (see the example above). We should avoid drawing the conclusion that because we might not think that even an independent life would be a worthwhile option for us, that it is not a worthwhile option for anyone in any society. This is not to say that it is impossible to make comparative value judgements about the values, morality and behaviour of different societies, but merely to accept that there may be ways of living a worthwhile life that are different from our own. Only if we were to insist that only an autonomous life could be a worthwhile one, would we be inclined to judge other kinds of life as non-worthwhile. We might, however, admit that even in this society we could lead independent or even non-independent lives if we had autonomously chosen to do so. We might, for example, autonomously decide to go into a religious order or become a professional soldier.

We have seen that an autonomous person can choose their life goals. But does this mean that they can choose *any* life goals? Some will be regarded as worthwhile in modern liberal democracies: adoption of a set of recognised values, having a satisfying and useful job, raising a family, working for charities, etc. These possibilities should be open to individuals and society would regard them as worthwhile. This does not mean that they are the only *legal* options but rather that most members of the society see them as possible constituents of a worthwhile life. But what about choices that are not considered to be worthwhile by any significant group within the society – for example, gambling, alcohol addiction, begging, a lifetime spent surfing? Notice that these are not actually illegal in most liberal democratic societies but nor are they considered to be constituents of a worthwhile life. Most societies do not forbid all activities that are considered to be non-worthwhile, although they will disapprove of them. Provided the alcoholic does not harm other people through driving while drunk, or does not finance his habit through theft, his activities are tolerated, meaning that the society is prepared to put up with them, considering that a greater harm would arise from forbidding them.

Most liberal societies are *strongly autonomous* in the weak sense that they tolerate a range of activities that are not worthwhile although not actually illegal, that is they are prepared to put up with them to a certain extent. Few societies are neutral towards non-worthwhile activities and fewer still actually encourage them. A society that only allowed people to pursue worthwhile activities would be *weakly autonomous*. Such a society would be regarded by many as very repressive, since there would be active discouragement or even criminal penalties for activities regarded as immoral or non-worthwhile. Notice that a society would have to be either strongly or weakly autonomous. If only worthwhile activities are allowed, then it is not possible to choose any non-worthwhile ones. However, it is a very different matter to ask whether or not education should *prepare* young people to exercise strong or weak autonomy with respect to their own lives. In particular, it does not follow that a society that is strongly autonomous should have, as an educational aim, that young people should be *prepared* to exercise strong autonomy. This is apparently a surprising conclusion since most philosophers of education take it largely for granted that if autonomy is an educational aim, then it should be interpreted as strong autonomy (White 1990; Norman 1994).

Concepts of the worthwhile and the reasonable

Let us examine the claim that strong autonomy should be an educational aim. If a society considers that it can tolerate strong autonomy, then one important variant of strong autonomy that it may wish to allow is the case where a minority community considers a certain range of life choices to be worthwhile which are not so considered by the rest of the society. They may be reasonable in the sense that they form the basis for co-operation with other groups within the society, but fail to match widely held conceptions of worthwhileness. Why should publicly funded education not prepare young people for reasonable lives, leaving them to make up their minds about what is or is not worthwhile?

The answer can be found in reflection on the conditions for autonomy. We have argued that preparation for autonomy involves gaining knowledge, self-knowledge and a range of abilities. School has only a limited amount of time in which to impart these. It cannot even hope to show children all the possibilities for a worthwhile life that may exist in their society. Some of these will have to be learned about outside school or maybe after formal schooling has been completed. It is fair to ask, 'Which should the school prioritise?' It is difficult to see how the answer could be otherwise than that, at the very least, the school should ensure that as many worthwhile options as possible were made available. There are no obvious grounds for prioritising any non-worthwhile choice over choices that are deemed to be worthwhile. The only reason for holding that one should, would be if one held that it was so important to offer children at least *some* non-worthwhile choices, that these options should take priority over some that are worthwhile. But whatever one thinks of this view, it is a much stronger one than the view that children should be allowed to prepare for non-worthwhile as well as worthwhile choices. In modern liberal democracies plenty of the former are available and there are ample opportunities to get acquainted with them. The idea that schools should give some of them priority as well seems bizarre. But even if they did, it would be another matter to actually *promote* some non-worthwhile choices.

In objection to the above, it might be said that there is no consensus on what are and what are not worthwhile options. But liberalism, at any rate, is not in a good position to maintain this, since it claims that an overlapping consensus about what is reasonable is the basis of the liberal state. It cannot claim that living in a liberal democratic society is not a worthwhile option, so at the very least, the way of life involved in a liberal society is worthwhile. That is why liberals have no qualms about prescribing civic education that underpins these principles. But we can grant that, within a liberal polity, some communities regard some options as worthwhile and others regard the same options as not worthwhile. But all this shows us is that, given that communities have the right to pursue their own conceptions of what is worthwhile within the framework of a liberal polity, they have the right to use the public schooling system to develop at least some of what they regard as worthwhile choices. This remains the case even if liberalism excludes any form of religious instruction from the schooling system. A religious community would still wish the state education system in their own community to introduce and promote options that were compatible with, or which supported, their own conceptions of the worthwhile.

Autonomy as a necessary condition of worthwhileness and its educational implications

If we assume that a necessary condition for living a worthwhile life in a liberal democratic society is to be autonomous, then it seems to follow that an education that failed to prepare one for autonomy should not be countenanced, on the grounds that it failed to prepare one for a worthwhile life. Notice that educational strong autonomists are in some difficulty with this, since they hold that one can be prepared for a possible non-worthwhile life. We have seen, however, that preparation for autonomy is complex, and that one can be prepared for many of the features necessary for the exercise of autonomous choice: self-mastery, self-knowledge, evaluative capacity, etc. without necessarily being fully prepared to make an autonomous choice. So many features of preparation for a non-autonomous life would be shared with preparation for an autonomous one. The key difference would lie in the capacity for choice of life plan that autonomy requires.

Does autonomous choice have to be conscious? Imagine someone who comes from a non-autonomy-promoting home or community background, but who has an autonomy-promoting education. Such a person could take a 'default option' of staying within their non-autonomy promoting community, without consciously *worrying* about whether or not they should. They would, however, still have been given meaningful alternatives from which to choose. These alternatives would have to be promoted as possible constituents of a worthwhile life in order to be meaningful, and would have to be presented in such a way that a young person would have some knowledge of what they involved and why some people might be attracted to them. We saw in the previous chapter how this could be regarded as a necessary feature of civic education in a public education system in a liberal democratic society. We also saw previously that civic and cultural education requires the development of a *critical capacity*, in order for both democracy and culture to flourish. We can say, then, that even an education that prepared some young people for a non-autonomous life would, in order to be properly accountable to the society, have to develop a good awareness of possible alternative forms of living a worthwhile life. Even if such a person decided to continue with the non-autonomous life favoured by their community, they would have been given the capacity to choose not to do so.

Should this be enough? Some might say that it is morally wrong and violates the rights of people to fail to explicitly educate them for autonomy, so that they are expected to make a choice. Thus, families might bring children up to believe certain moral principles without at the same time being invited to question them. Is it unjust to a child to bring them up in a particular system of religious beliefs, for example? One response would be to say 'yes' on the grounds that the children have a right to choose their own beliefs. We have already seen that the making of serious non-arbitrary choices is highly complex and presupposes a great deal of education before one arrives at such a point. The question remains as to whether it would be possible to make an autonomous choice as to what religion one should adopt if one had already been brought up in a particular religion. Clearly, meaningful alternatives would have to be available and a young person would have to have available accurate knowledge of such alternatives and the opportunity for meaningful engagement with them. It is far from clear that such conditions cannot be met in a pluralist society with the forms of civic education already argued for in the previous chapter. If this line of reasoning is correct, then it would follow that, subject to the constraints made above, it would be possible for someone to be brought up to be able to exercise conscious autonomous choice but choosing the values that they had, non-autonomously, been brought up with. There is a very significant difference between an upbringing in which one is seriously introduced to meaningful alternatives and one in which one is not. Once one does introduce a young person to meaningful alternatives, it is open to them to choose from among them, whether the parent wishes this or not.

One could say that people need to be able to choose a set of values including whether or not to adhere to a form of religious belief if one is to be autonomous. This involves some degree of engagement with religious practices and a realisation that there are alternatives to these, including the non-observance of any religion. A solution adopted by some education systems, which we discuss in Chapter 10, is to sanction faith schools for those parents who wish their children to be brought up in a religious way of life.

But there is a deeper issue at stake here. Liberals like Rawls are at pains to point out that the kind of individual self that a liberal society requires is not one that has no values or beliefs (Rawls 1993). It is only necessary that one be able to temporarily divest oneself of these in order to consider what political arrangements are reasonable. They hold this for a good reason; a self without values or beliefs is one that can have no conception of what is and what is not worthwhile for them. But in order to become a full self in this sense, one has to acquire values and beliefs at a time when one is not intellectually in a position to determine what values and beliefs one would like to acquire. Even the cherished liberal belief that one should be able to critically evaluate all beliefs, if this were a foundational belief for a child's education, would have to be inculcated without the child's consent. More generally, to be brought up within a community is to be brought up to acquire a set of values and beliefs, and this includes liberal communities. It seems, then, that education has to involve the inculcation of some values and beliefs. Far from being coercion, this practice is a necessary part of the acquisition of a rich enough sense of selfhood to be able to make significant choices in the future about the kind of person that one wishes to be.

Conclusion: the place of preparation for autonomy in education in a contemporary liberal democratic society

A society which has, as its central institutions, democratic government, a strong emphasis on individual rights, the defence of value pluralism and market economics, can hardly avoid promoting autonomy as an educational aim. This is not to say that the only worthwhile kind of life is an autonomous one in which one is free to choose one's political, moral, religious beliefs and one's vocation. In a society in which these central institutions have intrinsic value, or value in themselves, that is, where they are believed to be partially constitutive of a good life in that society, autonomy must itself have intrinsic value, since it is partially constitutive of living a worthwhile life in that kind of society that one has the capacity for autonomy.

The question of what kind of autonomy one should be brought up to is controversial and this chapter has discussed the main issues at stake. These can now be summarised. First, one cannot bring up children without bringing them up into some value beliefs. This is culpable if it is done in an immoral way, although it cannot be immoral of itself, although some people will regard the inculcation of some values as mistaken. Second, to be autonomous is to have a developed capacity for choice and for seeing through one's choices to successful conclusions; it does not necessarily involve an episode of deliberate conscious consideration of alternatives. Third, no community is under the obligation to bring children up to make choices that it does not consider worthwhile ones for any individual. Finally, the state has to take some account of what communities want as well as what is necessary to maintain the political institutions of the society, in deciding what should happen in publicly funded education. Each of these conclusions is controversial, but we believe that they are the most sustainable position for an educator committed to autonomy.

The development of autonomy has, we think, the following general implications for public education policy:

1 The role of the state in child-rearing is minimal. Subject to constraints of care and rationality, parents have the primary responsibility for children's social, moral and religious upbringing in those areas not covered by the school curriculum.
2 Schools should provide children with sufficient significant alternatives for them to be in a position to meaningfully engage with different vocational alternatives.
3 School-based religious education, whether faith-based or not, should present children with meaningful alternatives sufficient for them to have a degree of engagement with those alternatives should they choose to do so, provided those alternatives are thought to be worthwhile by significant communities within the polity.
4 Children should have the opportunity to develop mature and stable interests that will give them sufficient self-knowledge to make meaningful life-choices.

Questions for discussion

1 What are the main elements of autonomy?
2 What aspects of life should a young person have autonomous choices about?

3   Is it wrong to bring children up according to a particular system of moral or religious beliefs?
4   What should the role of local communities be in determining what is taught in schools?
5   How should children brought up in secular households be educated to make an autonomous choice about which religion, if any, to adopt?

Further reading

Autonomy is a really well-discussed topic in the philosophy of education and is also much discussed in political philosophy. Meira Levinson's *The Demands of Liberal Education* (Oxford, Oxford University Press, 2000) examines the concept of autonomy in the context of liberal political theory and draws out the consequences of the relationship between the two for both child-rearing and schooling. Harry Brighouse's *School Choice and Social Justice* (Oxford, Oxford University Press, 2000) is particularly concerned with the relationship between autonomy-promoting education and equality in schooling. An earlier book by Eamonn Callan, *Autonomy and Schooling* (Kingston, ONT, McGill Queen's University Press, 1993), covers some of the ground covered by Levinson and Brighouse, with particular emphasis on a conception of autonomy as self-mastery. Rousseau's (1910) *Emile* is perhaps the classic text for the development of the modern idea of autonomy. Rousseau's educational prescriptions are, however, both highly original and highly controversial. John White's *Education and the Good Life* (London, Routledge, 1990) is a good introduction to strong autonomy as an educational aim, while Richard Norman's 'I Did it My Way: Some Reflections on Autonomy', *Journal of Philosophy of Education*, 28, 1: 25–34 (1994) is a brief and accessible introduction to this position. Ruth Jonathan's *Illusory Freedoms* (Oxford, Blackwell, 1997) poses a more sceptical attitude to the liberal attitude to autonomy. Joseph Raz's *The Morality of Freedom* (Oxford, The Clarendon Press, 1986) is, among other things, an extended defence of weak autonomy in liberal societies. Christopher Winch's 'Strong Autonomy and Education', *Educational Theory*, 52, 1: 27–42 (2002) explores the question as to whether a public education system can sanction strong autonomy as an educational aim.

Chapter 8

Vocationalism, training and economics

We have seen throughout this book that education is for different purposes: individual fulfilment, membership of a democratic society and participation in work and economic life. In Chapter 6 we paid particular attention to the civic aspect of education and in Chapter 7 we took a detailed look at individual fulfilment. It is now time to consider preparation for work as a key aim of education. We begin by contrasting practical and vocational education and go on to consider the view that work is drudgery and that education should not prepare us for it. We argue, using examples from different societies, that this is a somewhat outdated view of much contemporary employment. The distinction between vocational and prevocational education is made in terms of what properly belongs to colleges and workplaces, on the one hand, and what properly belongs to schools, on the other. We then go on to survey the variety of forms of vocational education 'proper' and consider the large question of whether there are economic aims of education. This question is answered in the affirmative. Finally, we consider the role of work in contemporary societies.

Liberal, civic and vocational education

Vocational education is not an alternative to civic and liberal aspects of education, but complements it. Vocational education prepares young people to take part in the economic life of their society, both in order to 'earn a living' and, in a broader sense, to contribute to the well-being of the community. Vocational education is often derided and thought of as little more than a preparation for mindless drudgery. The main reason why this is thought to be the case is that paid work is wrongly taken always to consist of mindless drudgery for the great majority and to be fulfilling for only a lucky few. It follows from this perception that vocational education is, in fact, *training*, which is then wrongly thought of as a form of conditioning, which involves mindless responses to routine stimuli. Whether paid work can be worthwhile is a question that is too rarely asked.

On the other hand, if paid work can require skill and dedication and be a source of satisfaction to those who carry it out, then it should not be despised. Since it is likely that skilled and satisfying work requires a considerable degree of education, apprenticeship or training, then vocational education, in a broad sense, will play an essential role in preparing young people for paid work. Much of the evidence now available suggests that modern work is increasingly like this, despite considerable variations, even between developed countries. Rising rates of staying on at school, together with an increase in the numbers staying on for vocational courses beyond the school leaving age, contribute to this picture (Green *et al.* 1999). It is worth noting that many courses in higher education (roughly education beyond the qualification level reached by 18-year-olds) are vocational in the sense that they are explicitly designed for certain occupations. We will look at vocational education in this world in which paid work demands an increasingly skilled and knowledgeable workforce.

Practical and vocational education

Vocational education is often thought to be practical, concerned with the knowledge and technique necessary for 'getting things done' rather than for 'thinking' or 'contemplating'. However, one may get paid for thinking, for example, if one gets a job as a philosopher. Likewise, one may 'do something practical' and not get paid for it, for example, when one decorates one's own house or repairs one's car. Nevertheless, most jobs do assume a certain degree of practical ability, even most philosophers have to teach and need to be able to plan and think about their teaching activities.

In this sense, vocational education involves the acquisition of 'know how' and the kind of understanding derived from experience, as well as, in many cases, factual and theoretical knowledge. The traditional valuation of factual and theoretical over practical knowledge and experience is one reason why practical activities and practical education tend to be looked down on, more in some cultures than in others. But is this preference nothing more than an irrational and culturally induced prejudice? Our discussion of liberal and civic education gives reason for thinking that it is a prejudice. We argued that one form of liberal education involved acquaintance with the achievements of one's culture, while civic participation implied the ability to understand, make judgements about and participate in one's polity. Surely both liberal and civic education require a great deal of factual and theoretical knowledge?

We see no reason to deny this, but wish also to draw attention to another feature of liberal and civic education, which give them both a strongly practical aspect. We argued in Chapter 7 that a central aim of liberal education in modern societies is the development of individual autonomy, or the ability to form one's own plans for one's life and to carry them through. Lives involve different features which include: work, leisure, family and personal relationships, religion in some cases, and civic participation. Theoretical knowledge is insufficient for success in any of these areas of life and they all require some degree of practical mastery. The promotion of autonomy as a liberal aim of education has, ironically, a strong vocational implication. In our society, paid work is centrally important for a number of reasons. Unlike the eighteenth-century English gentry, very few of us have the ability to be self-supporting. We have to work for a living. Second, paid work occupies a very important role in our lives, quite apart from our need to work for a living. It is through work that we meet other people, pursue at least some of our interests and exercise some of our most prized abilities. Third, being a successful worker is important to our self-esteem and the recognition that we get from others. This is not surprising, given the previous two reasons. One might of course argue that paid work has too much importance in our lives, to such an extent that we have ceased to value unpaid work such as raising a family. We have a lot of sympathy for this objection and acknowledge the importance of balance in people's lives, but even when this has been acknowledged, for most people, respected, fulfilling and well-paid work remains a central life goal. A liberal educator who takes autonomy seriously should acknowledge the importance of preparing children to make good choices about work-related aims. On this view, therefore, vocational education in some sense is central to education for autonomy.

The point is not so obvious in relation to civic education but is still significant. Civic education at its best enables children and young people to work with others and to make decisions as participants in the political society and the civic institutions such as businesses, trade unions, etc. that accompany it. Civic education should prepare young people for all aspects of civic life, including those that are work-related, such as issues to do with disputes over pay and working conditions, the overall direction of the economy and the control of the enterprises in which they work.

We can see then that vocational education, broadly conceived, need not lie outside the wider stream of education. But doubts might still remain. We saw that liberal and civic education requires various abilities and dispositions as well as factual knowledge. In order to choose whether or not to work for a living and, if so, which kind of work to pursue, will involve personal self-mastery, self-knowledge and the ability to evaluate the consequences of decisions. 'But surely', the objection might go, 'these are important *preliminaries* before one starts work. They are to do with preparation for a working life, not for education in how to work itself.' Someone making this objection might continue in the following vein: 'Work involves submission to the authority of one's superiors and training in the carrying out of humdrum routines, or at the most, practice of a set of limited skills. Submission to authority, the carrying out of humdrum routines and the practice of limited skills are not worthwhile objects of an educational experience. Therefore, preparation for them is not a proper part of education, it belongs to work training' (see, for example, Adam Smith ([1776], 1981); Barrow (1981); Dearden (1984)).

We think that this is a powerful objection to what we have so far argued for, but it is one that can be fully answered. The first point to bear in mind is that preparation for choosing where to work is different from learning how to work. The second is not a proper part of *school education*, while the ability to make a meaningful choice in the first sense is, as part of the development of *autonomy*. In addition, preparation for becoming a citizen who is also a worker is a proper part of *civic education*. The second point to bear in mind is that learning how to work is a proper part of education, although not part of school-based education. The third point is that we must be very careful to present a realistic and non-stereotypical account of what paid work involves. Nearly all work, both paid and unpaid, involves a certain degree of submission to authority, humdrum routine and the practice of limited skills. If this is all there was to it, work-based vocational preparation would involve little more than low-level training and nothing else. There are many jobs of this kind, but we must be careful not to jump to the conclusion of Adam Smith concerning the nature of most work.

> The man whose whole life is spent in performing a few simple operations, of which the effects are, perhaps, always the same, or very nearly the same, has no occasion to exert his understanding, or to exercise his invention in finding out expedients for removing difficulties which never occur. He naturally loses, therefore, the habit of such exertion, and generally becomes as stupid and ignorant as it is possible for a human creature to become.
>
> (Smith [1776], (1981), Book V, S.785–786)

Smith wrote both as an observer and as a propagandist for the extreme fragmentation of work tasks into small unskilled components, on the grounds of economic efficiency and productivity. His ideas were taken up in the line management and time and motion techniques advocated by Frederick Taylor (1911) and the mass-production conveyor-based manufacturing pioneered by Henry Ford. Karl Marx (1887) largely followed Smith's predictions as to the nature of work in industrial capitalism. While there is no doubt that the extensive use of unskilled labour was central to the development of industrial societies, especially the UK and the USA, we must be very careful not to adopt an over-simplified picture, nor to assume that what might have been true of the late nineteenth and most of the twentieth century is still largely true today.

There is now increasing evidence that many of the older and newer industrialised countries are bent on following a 'high-skill' route to economic competitiveness (Ashton and Green 1996; Crouch et al. 1999). This involves competing in markets for high specification, high quality goods and services and means that the workforce itself is both highly skilled and well paid (so that they can buy this kind of good). Highly skilled workers in the modern context are people who have received a good general education and who have then entered an occupation in which a range of specialised but related skills are required. Typically, these skills may involve manual abilities linked to a certain degree of craft and/or technical knowledge, the ability to take responsibility for one's work, to work in teams with colleagues and to be able to update relevant knowledge (Hodgson 1999; Prais 1995). In some countries, of which Germany is a notable example, workers are expected to take part in the governance of their firms through a system of industrial democracy (Streeck 1992).

For example, we find that the German system requires that trainees in the construction industry spend the first year of training between the college and a training centre studying a common course for all construction trainees irrespective of the particular trade which they have entered with their employer. In the Netherlands, the training for a skilled carpenter, which is the dominant trade in the Dutch construction industry, involves the study of applied mathematics, physics and mechanics in modules devised by the Ministry of Education. Students also spend a day a week in the college system studying a curriculum that includes a foreign language and environmental studies (Clarke and Wall 2000).

We can see from the above examples that the view of most, if not all, work as routine, unskilled drudgery is no longer taken as accurate by some states. In many industrial societies, work has become a complex mix of manual and intellectual skills, together with applied theoretical knowledge. Unless one takes the view that work is, of itself, drudgery, it seems difficult to maintain that it *must* be as unattractive as it is often made out to be. Naturally there are, in modern societies still many kinds of job which do not afford the opportunities mentioned above. Some developed societies still persist in taking the low skills route to competitiveness, the UK and, to some extent, the USA are examples of this (Ashton and Green 1996). But the decision to opt for a high skill or a low skill strategy is, in the end, a political as much as an economic one and, as such, part of the civic responsibility of the citizens of that society.

To summarise, it is not obvious that paid work is nothing more than drudgery. Many philosophers and social theorists have seen work as a typically human activity involving the exercise of one's active powers in a social context (Weil 1958). As such, fulfilling work is one of the possible constituents of a worthwhile life and the subject of choice for an autonomous individual. Vocational education itself, preparing for a specific job or occupation, can be a complex and detailed introduction to a demanding and fulfilling aspect of adult existence, which has, in addition a strong civic and individual dimension. It is only when we think of paid work as routine drudgery where little skill or initiative is required, only training in obedience and the following of routines, that we are entitled to think of vocational education with the degree of contempt which has often been reserved for it in our society.

Jobs and occupations

One of the most common confusions about work is that between a *job*, on the one hand, and an *occupation*, on the other. The term *task* refers to specific activities that someone may undertake, such as sawing wood or assembling a frame. *Job*, on the other hand, refers to the individual specific employment contract to work for a particular firm. To say that so and so's *job* is to install kitchens is to specify a range of *tasks* to perform as part of their employment contract for a particular firm. 'Occupation' refers to the category of labour that carries out such work; a kitchen fitter will also belong to the *occupation* of carpenter or joiner.

It should be obvious that one could be employed in a series of different jobs, each of which involved an array of tasks within the same occupation, for instance, in the case of a carpenter/joiner as a suspended ceiling fitter, a first or second fix carpenter, a furniture maker, shop fitter, or exhibition erector – to name but a few. It is important not to leap to the conclusion that someone has moved through more than one occupation merely because they have changed jobs on successive occasions. In this sense, an occupation is a formally recognised social category. An occupation has a regulative structure concerning training, qualification, promotion and the range of knowledge, both practical and theoretical, that is required to undertake the range of tasks that fall within it. Occupations such as teaching and medicine are occupations in this sense because their recognition is rooted in the regulative structure of society. Some such occupations, which typically require qualification at least to degree level, gain the status of *professions* for reasons that may have to do with social and political pressure (Winch and Clarke 2003).

Much of the talk about the dynamic and fluid nature of modern society ignores this important distinction. Someone may well change his or her job several times in a working life. It is much less likely that they will change their occupations more than once or twice, for the simple reason that entry to an occupation usually requires years of difficult preparation. It is only if one is an unskilled labourer or casual worker whose job tasks do not fit into a recognised occupational category that it makes sense to talk in this way. If one takes the view of work suggested here, it should be obvious that societies should try to minimise the range of unskilled and casual work that they expect to be done, although of course they cannot eliminate it entirely. Some people will continue to need 'Mcjobs' either on a temporary basis or because they are unable or unwilling to enter an occupation.

Occupations, then, have a more or less established place in society. In addition to being kind of ways in which people earn their living, they also serve the needs of and have an impact on the rest of society. Some of these occupations serve 'life and death' necessities: medicine and farming, for example. Without doctors or farmers we would die. Others serve what Carr (1999) has called 'civic necessities', those that contribute to the worthwhileness of life. Into this category come teachers, railway workers, builders, shopkeepers and clergy, for example. Other occupations again address relatively trivial needs, but nevertheless contribute to the overall quality of life, such as restaurateurs and hairdressers. It is important to realise that occupations have an impact, not just on their clients, but also on the broader society.

Prevocational education and autonomy

So far we have argued that vocational education has a central role in preparation for life and, as such, it should be taken as seriously as the other two main aspects of education, liberal and civic. But we must not lose sight of the distinction mentioned above. On the one hand is the *choosing* of an occupation, on the other, is the *preparation* for that occupation. Young people will usually begin to get some idea of what kind of occupation they would like to enter by the time they are 14 years old. They can only do this if they have some information concerning what is available to them. But they also need to know if they have the potential ability, temperament and long-term interest to enter the occupation. Schools have a key role in helping children to make such choices, but there are some difficulties as well.

It is not just enough to be *informed* about an occupation in order to be able to make a choice about whether or not to enter it, one needs to have some *experience* of it as well. Only through some experience of what it is like to work in the occupation will young people know whether the occupation suits them and whether they are suited to it. But how can a school provide such experience? This difficulty can be partly overcome in three ways. The first is to provide some of the experience within the school curriculum, by providing vocational subjects with the appropriate teachers, equipment and buildings. This involves a degree of specialisation within the school system. The second is to provide links between schools and workplaces that allow young people some experience of what life is like in the working environment of the occupation that they are considering. The third is to provide them with specialist career assessment and advice. Ideally, a school should be capable of providing all these things.

It is useful to recall the discussion of autonomy, where it was argued that young people need to know which choices are worthwhile ones and will suit their abilities and temperaments. They also need to have the self-mastery to pursue a choice through some doubts and difficulties. The ability to make autonomous choices presupposes some knowledge, some ability to reason and a degree of emotional maturity. Prevocational education should have the aim of giving young people such knowledge, both of occupations and of themselves, and of providing them with sufficient opportunities to explore the difficulties as well as the pleasures of a potential occupational choice, so that they are capable of making an informed decision. This is a demanding role for schools, but one that is vital to the well-being of young people and of the society that they live in.

The policy implications of an argument of prevocational education are considerable. In particular, the requirement that young people gain some 'hands-on' experience of a potential occupation provides doubts in the minds of some. Should schools specialise the curriculum after, say, the ages of 13 or 14 in order to provide these opportunities? Doesn't this mean segregating young people and depriving some of them of a proper liberal education? If one does make this choice, what are the resource implications? Do specialist teaching staff with experience of the occupation need to be hired? Should separate specialist schools with appropriate equipment and buildings be provided? How many different groups of occupations can one cater to in a vocationally oriented secondary school system? These are all difficult policy questions which can be addressed in different ways.

The last two are essentially practical and financial questions, but the first clearly concerns the *justice* of educational specialisation. We have already argued forcefully in Chapter 2 for the desirability of a common curriculum in the earlier and middle stages of schooling, and we would also argue that in vocational routes there should continue to be strong elements of academic education provided as part of prevocational education. Indeed, as we have already noted, many countries continue academic education into post-school vocational education itself. It is essential that children are provided with the basic competence to be independent within their society, with sufficient cultural knowledge to understand its history, geography and politics and with a knowledge of the science and technology that underpin its culture. We have also, in Chapter 6, made out a strong case for moral, personal and civic education.

But we have also argued strongly for autonomy as a key liberal educational aim, and although being autonomous does not solely mean the ability to choose an occupation, it is a very significant aspect of such a choice and requires a complex preparation. Prevocational education, therefore, is a key element of liberal education for many young people who wish to follow an occupational choice beyond the minimum school leaving age. In this sense, it is a central part of the role of the secondary school in catering, not just for young people with strong academic inclinations, but also for those with strong vocational ones.

The various kinds of vocational education

We now move to vocational education 'proper'. As suggested above, school is not the appropriate place for this. One can only learn about an occupation and the jobs and tasks associated with it, if one is in a position to gain intimate and first-hand experience of the range of tasks associated with it. Evidently the workplace is the most suitable location in which to do this. However, it is, by itself, inadequate and one of the difficulties in addressing this issue is precisely the relationship between 'on' and 'off' job elements of vocational education. In mediaeval Europe there developed strong occupational associations known as 'guilds' whose role was to practise, regulate, negotiate for and develop the occupation, as well as, crucially, to regulate entry into it and to form future workers. In order to do this, the guilds developed a form of vocational education known as 'apprenticeship'. Apprenticeship not only involved a prolonged engagement with the techniques and virtues of the practice of occupational tasks, but also involved induction into the occupation as a way of life, which included its own ideals and practices. Apprenticeship was, thus, much more than technical vocational education, it was also, in a sense, an introduction to a way of life and a process of character formation (Ainley and Rainbird 1999).

Although there is some continuity between mediaeval and modern forms of apprenticeship, notably in the way in which apprentices are taken on as cadet workers rather than as students, there are obviously also huge differences. The degree of control exerted by the master and the guild over the apprentice is much diminished. In its place have come state regulation and assessment procedures, together with greater flexibility of employment opportunities. It is also important to note that in the contemporary work environment, occupational boundaries are more changing and fluid than they were in the mediaeval period. Nevertheless, through the fact that the apprentice was bound to a master tradesman for a period and the fact that the guilds prescribed the length and nature of occupational formation, apprenticeship was a form of 'total' educational experience, which was much more than technical instruction. Much of what was learned was also learned outside the workshop itself.

In contemporary conditions, with the development of technique based on science and technology, it is necessary to provide entrants into an occupation with extended general education, applied theoretical knowledge particularly relevant to the occupation and the ability to practise the integration of theoretical knowledge and the safe implementation of technique outside the pressures of the workplace. The occupational entrant also needs a period of *probationary practice* in order to gain confidence, to consolidate technique and to gain a proper sense of responsibility when working with other people. It should, therefore, be clear that vocational education for skilled work is a complex matter which requires well-thought-out pathways and forms of oversight over those pathways. The elements of theoretical and factual knowledge now required by many occupations mean that the classroom is an important venue for at least some of this vocational education. The element of simulation in turn requires that workshops are available for the safe and incremental practice of technique, while the probationary workplace element means that there are robust forms of supervision, recording and assessment available within the workplace itself. Vocational education for occupations that require a degree of skill and knowledge thus requires structures that integrate these three elements. While in many cases the workplace is not sufficient to provide the range of educational experiences required, neither is the classroom and college-based workshop adequate to provide the full range of practical experience necessary (Clarke and Winch, forthcoming).

Different societies have dealt with this complexity in different ways. Some have preferred to retain strong elements of Taylorist practice and relatively low levels of skill, thus avoiding the need for large-scale complex forms of vocational education (to some extent the USA and the UK have followed this route for some occupations). Others have concentrated vocational education within the upper years of post-compulsory schooling, often within specialist schools or areas of schools (France and Japan represent this tendency). Others again have used apprenticeship together with enhanced general and technical education based in specialist colleges (Germany, Austria and Switzerland represent this model, together with the UK for a restricted range of occupations, see Green *et al.* 1999, for an account of the different formal routes). Yet others place a lot of reliance on informal family networks based on regionally specialised industries, parts of Italy have such a pattern (Crouch *et al.* 1999). Despite the convergence of many societies on the need for enhanced skill levels, one striking feature of adaptation to this need has been the *diverse* ways in which it has continued to be met. Even countries sharing a common geographical region and a lot of common history, such as Western Europe, show a striking diversity in the ways in which they deal with vocational education, in many cases drawing on well-established historical traditions, of which apprenticeship is a good example in some contemporary societies.

Vocational education is thus far more than a matter of drilling or training for a restricted range of unskilled tasks. It involves induction into an occupation with its own place in society and its own ideals and traditions. It requires a complex combination of factual, theoretical and practical knowledge, not to mention the practice of specific occupational virtues. The increasing pace of economic competition among developed countries and between developed and developing countries has ensured that, for better or for worse, vocational education will continue to occupy a central and growing place for some time to come. It is becoming increasingly common for young people not following an academic route into higher education to continue with some form of post-compulsory vocational education. Corresponding with this is the increasing scarcity of unskilled jobs (although the UK and the USA are, in some respects, exceptions to this trend). Catering for the employment and social needs of the small minority of completely unskilled is likely to become a pressing social, political and economic problem for our societies.

The economic aims of education

Up to this point, we have largely considered vocational education from the point of *individual* aims of education. One of the complaints often levelled against vocational education as *education* is that it subordinates the needs of the individual to those of society. We hope to have shown in the previous sections that this can be an unfounded view, if prevocational and vocational education are properly conducted. However, there is little doubt that there is a connection between education in general, and vocational education in particular, and economic development and it is also true that more people are attaching importance to the economic aims of education. How should we respond to these concerns? Our initial reaction is that there is not necessarily any incompatibility between economic development *as such* and individual development. Much depends, however, on the way in which the economy of a society is conducted.

There are two broad strategies for running the economy of an industrialised society – as a *high skill equilibrium* (HSE) or as a *low skill equilibrium* (LSE) (Ashton and Green 1996). In an HSE, highly skilled and highly paid workers produce high specification and relatively expensive goods and services, which are sold to relatively affluent consumers, who are, mostly, the highly paid workers themselves. An HSE is a virtuous cycle in which high quality products are made and consumed by well-paid workers doing satisfying work. Movement to an HSE has the further long-term economic advantage of giving developed economies a competitive edge and a heightened ability to adapt in a world where more and more countries are competing in similar areas.

Economies can also be run in the contrary way, where poorly paid, low-skilled workers produce cheap but low-specification and low-quality goods and services tailored to the budgets of unskilled, low-paid workers. Such is a low skill equilibrium (LSE). Economies run as LSEs can be profitable. What they cannot do is provide satisfying work, worthwhile products or long-term economic security through built-in adaptability to changing economic circumstances. There is now considerable evidence that much of the UK economy is run as an LSE, while our economic partners and competitors in Europe have, in the main, followed the HSE route.

Moving from an LSE to an HSE is an example of a co-ordination problem, in which a certain state of affairs, to the advantage of everyone, cannot be readily achieved by individual action. In particular, it looks like an example of a 'prisoner's dilemma' problem where the dominant strategy of individual employers in an LSE is to remain in one (see further discussion in Chapter 9). A prisoner's dilemma is a form of co-ordination situation where it is the dominant strategy of each player to opt for a course that produces an outcome that is not the best that all players could obtain. One important aspect of the transition from an LSE to an HSE is to develop a skilled workforce.

In this case, all employers could gain more if all employees were to train, although all employers would incur the cost of training their own employees. However, if an employer were to train while other employers did not, that employer would incur the cost of training but fail to recoup any of the benefits, since the other employers would use the saving gained from not training to 'poach' the trained employees from the employer who trained. Naturally, the optimum outcome for any single employer would be not to train while all the others did. However, since all employers can work out the outcomes of each possible course of action, it is unlikely that any would want to train. The only way to ensure that all employers trained their employees would be to provide some incentive to do so outside the strict confines of the game itself. For example, if all employers were made to bear the costs of training their employees, then they would all have an incentive to train them, since they would all recoup those costs and would not be subject to poaching from other employers, since there would no longer be a shortage of skilled workers.

It should be obvious that there are considerable social advantages to running a mature economy as an HSE. In terms of our account of well-being being partly constituted by the exercise of our active powers in worthwhile activities, an HSE has clear advantages over an LSE, just because people have the opportunity to exercise their active powers, to engage in co-operation with others in the workplace and to exert a measure of control over the workplace. It should also be fairly clear that HSEs require a strong degree of *initial* vocational education, as well as continuing learning as part of occupational development.

In the first place, occupational choice requires the careful sort of prevocational education that we have advocated. Second, high skill jobs are usually situated *within* occupations, and, as we saw, induction into an occupation requires extended preparation in order that the skills and knowledge mastered are not just those associated with a small range of tasks, but with the full range of tasks to be found within an occupation, together with the knowledge and understanding of the place of the occupation in the wider industrial sector and within society at large. In addition, technological change has tended to reduce the number of occupational categories and, at the same time, to broaden those that remain. This has had the effect of requiring the *multiskilling* of workers within that occupation.

This leads us to consideration of the relationship between education and economic policy. If moving to an HSE is a co-ordination problem, as we have argued, then the government has to take the initiative to ensure that it is in the interests of employers to train their workers. Such policies could take the form of a levy or training tax, or a licence to practise in an occupation conditional on gaining a qualification. Ultimately, vocational education policy is a deeply political matter as it affects the fundamental interests of employers and employees and may involve overriding the perceived interests of one or both of these groups, at least in the short term. Agreement about such issues is much easier to obtain when the main parties can agree upon what the main direction of economic development should be, much less easy to obtain when they cannot.

Vocational education and the good life: the end of work?

One objection to what we have argued for in this chapter is that it places too much emphasis on work as a component of the good life. We have, it is true, argued that satisfying work forms an essential part of the well-being of most people in our kind of society. But this does not imply that we are completely satisfied with the work–life balance or that there are not serious things wrong with the way in which we form priorities. All our argument requires is that a good working life is central to well-being for most people and that therefore a worthwhile education should prepare these people for it. But of course this is not the only thing that education should prepare us for: we have drawn attention to the importance of being able to come to some assessment of one's values and the moral, personal and civic aspects of life. But we can go further than this and say that the perspective that we have set out is quite consistent with the view that people work excessive hours, that they are not allowed to retire early enough if they wish and, above all, that we tend to look with a certain degree of contempt on *unpaid* forms of work, such as charitable work and, above all, raising a family. The contemporary absence of a 'living wage' which allows one partner to work to support his or her family means that it is nearly impossible for families to devote one person to full-time child care, when many people want that option. One solution that appeals to us is to allow the member of a family who wishes to spend time out of the labour market a basic income so that they can do so with a degree of dignity and without condemning their family to hardship. This could be accompanied with educational credits so that someone who made such a choice would be able to maintain and enhance their skills in order to re-enter the labour market when they saw fit. Such a scheme would also allow the basic income to be drawn when a certain amount of part-time hours were worked so that child-carers need not feel themselves to be isolated from the wider society. This is one way in which the overwhelming pull that work has on us, both morally and financially could be reduced.

Questions for further discussion

1 Is work an important part of life?
2 Can one really be autonomous at work? Discuss with examples.
3 Should schools prepare young people for work?
4 Can one only learn about work properly while learning 'on the job'?
5 Does the exercise of skill provide fulfilment? Should work provide this kind of fulfilment?

Further reading

Vocational education is a wide-ranging and complex field, in which philosophical, economic and historical issues are intertwined. Sadly, the area is underdeveloped in philosophical terms. A very good, but neglected, introduction is Harold Entwistle's *Education, Work and Leisure* (London, Routledge, 1970). A substantial work, which covers policy-making in the UK from a philosophical perspective is Richard Pring's *Closing the Gap: Liberal Education and Vocational Preparation* (London, Hodder and Stoughton, 1995). Christopher Winch's *Education, Work and Social Capital* (London, Routledge, 2000) is an extended explanation and defence of a liberal conception of vocational education. His *New Labour and the Future of Training* (London, Philosophy of Education of Great Britain, 2000), situates these arguments within a UK policy context. A contrasting view, based on the premise that in contemporary post-industrial societies, paid work is due to become largely obsolete, can be found in John White's *Education and the End of Work* (London, Kogan Page, 1997). Issues to do with the relationship between occupation, job and vocational education are discussed in David Carr, 'Professional Education and Professional Ethics', *Journal of Applied Philosophy*, 16, 1: 33–46 (1999), and Christopher Winch and Linda Clarke, '"Front-Loaded" Vocational Education Versus Lifelong Learning: A Critique of Current UK Government Policy', *Oxford Review of Education*, 29, 2: 239–252 (2003). Entwistle's book provides a good discussion of prevocational education. One area in which interesting work has been done is that of work-related learning. See, for example, Paul Hager's 'Know-how and Workplace Practical Judgment', *Journal of Philosophy of Education*, 34, 2: 281–296 (2000) and Gerard Lum, 'Where's the Competence in Competence-based Education and Training?', *Journal of Philosophy of Education*, 33, 3: 403–418 (1999), and Robert Dearden, 'Education and Training', *Westminster Studies in Education*, 7: 57–66 (1984). There is, of course, a vast range of empirical material related to vocational education and the interested reader is encouraged to pursue the other references in this chapter for access to this material.

Chapter 9

Markets, politics and education

In the Introduction, we drew attention to the problem of *accountability* or how those responsible for providing a service can be asked to justify what they have done with the resources provided for that service. In Chapter 5 we discussed this in relation to assessment. One of the problems with the provision of education is that it may not be responsive to the needs of those who use it, parents and their children. In a state educational monopoly, parents have no choice but to send their children to state schools. Very often, they have little or no choice as to *which* schools they can send their children. Even where the state does not enjoy a monopoly, it is impossible for most parents to pay the fees necessary to educate their children outside the state system. And yet there may be some good reasons why the state should not have such a power to dictate where and how children should be educated. This chapter examines the arguments for allowing market forces rather than the state to govern educational provision. It examines the concept of a market and then looks at how a market in educational provision would work. This leads to a consideration of whether the aim of education systems is to provide education or educational opportunities and it is argued that the former is the proper business of publicly funded education. The nature of educational goods are examined and the importance of education as a positional good is emphasised. The chapter then goes on to consider: who the consumer of education is, the alleged benefits of educational vouchers, the question of whether educational markets promote or impede educational equality and, finally, whether they are capable of providing diversity in educational provision.

One issue, highlighted by the economist Adam Smith, is that a teacher paid solely by the state 'would soon learn to neglect his business'. Smith supposed that if teachers were to be guaranteed an income by the state, they would have no incentive to provide a proper service. The only way in which parents can ensure that they will is by paying them according to their performance in educating their children. In such a system, good teachers will be well paid and bad teachers will be poorly paid. If we further assume that the best schools will be those with the best teachers, the higher pay that good teachers attract will mean that the best schools have the best paid teachers. Although the education provided by these schools will be the best, it will also be the most expensive.

But there is another issue besides efficiency. If the state controls education, even if it runs it with the best intentions and with the greatest possible degree of efficiency, there is always a danger that it will educate in a way that does not correspond to the wishes of parents. For example, parents may wish their children to have a religious upbringing, or they may wish to educate them to run a business. Neither of these possibilities may be available in a state-funded system. How can parents exert their influence to get the kind of education that they want? As we saw, even without a state monopoly, it may simply be too expensive for parents to provide, out of their own resources, the kind of education that they want their children to have. One possible solution to these difficulties is to provide a market in education.

What is a market?

At its simplest, a market is a location where buyers and sellers are brought together to exchange goods. Ideally, buyers and sellers should be instantly aware of all prices at which goods are offered (prices) and of all offers from potential customers (offers). The information should allow buyers and sellers to adjust prices and offers until the market 'clears', that is, all offers are accepted. The most obvious example of a market is a country vegetable fair where stallholders display their goods and buyers can inspect the offerings of different stall holders. They can also 'haggle' about the price. From the point of view of the seller, the price must reflect the labour put into the product, together with a profit. The price will also reflect the demand for the product, which will depend in turn on the competition among sellers and the number of buyers. *Scarcity* as well as the cost of labour inputs will determine price. From the buyers' point of view, it is important that the goods on offer correspond to their wants and that the goods are offered at an affordable price. A further important factor is that the buyer needs to have the knowledge to determine whether the goods on offer are of the right *quality*. There is no point in buying a worn-out horse or a 'clocked' car, even if the price is attractive and you need transport. In our simple model of a vegetable market, buyers and sellers are able to inspect offers and prices because they are near in space. But of course, the same principle can work if prices and offers are made available in other ways, for example, in print or electronically. This is the way in which, for example, the stock market works. In the case of the stock market, the quality of the product is sometimes assessed by a specialist called an 'analyst' who has researched the quality of a firm's business.

This is an idealised version of markets, of course. In practice, even in a vegetable market, instant awareness of offers and prices is not available, let alone in more spatially distributed markets. Neither is an accurate assessment of quality. The economist's idealised version of a market looks like something that works very well in theory but which does not correspond to reality. If this is so, it is doubtful whether economic theory has much to do with actual market practice. For this reason, some economists have adopted the 'Austrian' view of markets (so named because the idea originates with the Austrian econ- omist, Ludwig von Mises). In the Austrian model, buyers and sellers do not become instantly aware of all offers and prices. Instead, they become aware of prices and offers in their vicinity. However, this information spreads gradually throughout the market and affects the behaviour of buyers and sellers in other parts of the market. Thus, if low demand in one part of the market leads to a lowering of prices, buyers and sellers in other parts of the market get to hear of this and, to avoid buyers moving on, sellers in this part of the market adjust their prices to the new situation. Buyers also develop what is sometimes called 'tacit' knowledge of the goods on offer. By repeated inspection and comparison of offers they come to know something about the quality of what is offered rel- ative to its price and this knowledge is factored into their eventual purchasing decision.

One final point. Markets can be applied to the exchange of all kinds of goods and services. Vegetables, cars and horses are obvious examples. Shares are more abstract, but still a kind of tradeable good, because they are permanent even if not tangible. However, services can also be sold in the market, even though a service is neither tangible nor permanent. Not everything can be traded. For example, I can sell my shirt which is a commodity, but not my height, which is an inseparable part of me.

Markets in education

Given the problems of choice and accountability mentioned earlier, a market solution for education is quite attractive. It promises, in the first instance, to deal with disagreements concerning the aims of education. Once the state with- draws from the apparently impossible task of catering for the educational aims of all groups, then each group that has distinct aims can set up their own system of schools and colleges. If, for example, religiously-minded parents do not want their children to be educated in a secular system, then they are entitled to set up religious schools. The second advantage bestowed by a market approach is the answer it gives to the question of *accountability*. A market-based education system is based on exchanges between suppliers and purchasers. If purchasers do not like what is on offer, they do not have to buy it or they can withdraw their custom. There is no need for complicated systems of inspection to ensure that schools keep up to the mark. One interesting point, to which we will return, is whether or not *assessment* is needed as an indicator of the worthwhileness of what is on offer. It will be recalled that purchasers need to know, not just the availability and the price, but also its *quality*. How this is assessed is an issue when evaluating the market proposal for education. Finally, a market system will be flexible and quick to respond to changes in demand. Unpopular schools will close and popular ones will take their place. A market system of education promises to deal with some of the really difficult issues underlying the provision of education.

The aims of education revisited: to educate or to provide educational opportunities?

To begin with, we need to be sure about *what* exactly is being offered in a market-based educational system. If education is not a commodity, then evidently it cannot be offered on the market. We saw in Chapter 1 that a general definition of education is that it is a preparation for life. Being prepared for life is something that happens to an individual; it is, if you like, an individual achievement, something personal to whoever is educated. If I become educated, I cannot sell you my education, anymore than I can sell you my height. So it looks as if a market in education is a non-starter, since education is not a tradeable commodity. One response is to claim that the proper aim of educational institutions is not to provide education as such, but to provide educational *opportunities*. Opportunities are the kinds of thing that can be bought and sold, therefore it makes sense to talk of a market in educational opportunities. We had a brief look at this claim in Chapter 5 in relation to assessment issues. The question now arises, 'Do we mean by education a *preparation* for life, or the *opportunity* to prepare for life?' The way in which education is generally talked about suggests that it is something that one achieves, not an opportunity to achieve something. To take a particularly striking example, if I offer to educate your child morally, you would expect me to get your child to understand the difference between right and wrong, to do what is right and to avoid doing what is wrong. You would *not* merely expect me to provide the opportunities for the child to be good. You would not be satisfied if I handed your child back to you, as a delinquent, with the reasoning that I gave him every opportunity to become good, but he chose not to take those opportunities.

So it is implausible to say that education is just about offering opportunities. Nevertheless, the advocate of markets could reply that all that schools can realistically offer is the opportunity to become educated, they cannot *make* people become educated. Up to a point this is true. However, it is generally expected that schools will exert considerable pressure on pupils to learn to be good, to read, count and write, and so on, and that such pressure is justified, since to fail to be good, literate or numerate is not just a personal disaster for the child, but also for society, which runs the risk of having to cope with a criminal, illiterate and innumerate population. So it looks as if some educational marketeers are committed to taking up a very strong position on the rights of children to reject the education that is offered to them.

We now need to examine what it means to offer educational opportunities to someone. The obvious answer is that these are opportunities to acquire knowledge, attitudes and skills. It is natural then to suppose that the accountability function in markets is exercised through an assessment of the extent to which pupils have actually learned. Strangely, however, this is not an option that the market theorist can take up. For, as we saw in Chapter 5, what assessment evaluates is the extent to which someone has *learned*, not the extent to which they have been *offered opportunities*. It is no surprise, therefore, to find a market theorist claiming that the way in which to assess educational opportunities is to look at the playground, assess school facilities and to ask the child how they got on at school (Tooley 1998, p. 273). The obvious objection to this version of accountability is that the expectations of the market theorist and the parent who pays for education are wildly out of kilter. As we saw, parents would be aggrieved if it were explained to them that their ignorant or delinquent child had nevertheless been offered excellent opportunities which they had refused to take up. This view of what is offered in educational markets is, therefore, an absurdity and must be rejected, together with the idea that education is a kind of commodity.

It follows, then, that if we are to make sense of markets in education, we must take seriously the idea that what is offered is in some sense a *preparation for life*. Thus, the 'customer' for education is the parent or guardian, not the child. Children, especially young ones, will not have a clear view of the best way in which to prepare for life. In an educational market, parents pay for at least part of the upbringing of their children and they will take a view on the success or otherwise of that education in terms of achievements determined through assessment and through less measurable factors such as social skill, confidence and poise. All this implies that commitment to a school is a long-term process, since to frequently change one's school is to interrupt the process for which the parent has paid. This tilts the balance of power towards schools, which know that once a parent has committed to what they have to offer, it is not so easy to move away. But the balance of power rests with schools rather than parents in other ways as well.

In order to see this, it is necessary to examine more closely what good education is. In one sense it is something *substantial*: gaining values, knowledge, skill and confidence are all useful in life. However, education is also what is called a 'positional' good. This means that the value of one's education depends to some extent on its *prestige*. Just as a runner who wins a race enjoys more prestige than the second runner-up who, in turn, enjoys more prestige than those who come behind, so the holder of a high-status education enjoys more social kudos than one who enjoys a lower-status education. It is important to note that this is manifested not just through exam results but also through the kind of confidence that may be conveyed through the knowledge that one has had a prestigious education. This confidence is heightened if one of the assets of the school is the network of social contacts that it gives rise to in the adult world (the 'old school tie' phenomenon). The school, therefore, can be the gatekeeper to social prestige and success, not merely through the cognitive and moral benefits it gives, but also through the fact that it is the school that it is. Just as there can only be one winner of a race, so the positions that can be granted by education in a particular school are distributed so that the holding of a position by one person excludes another from holding the same. This limits the number of children that can benefit from education in particular schools and means that there is fierce competition to enter them. This puts high-status schools in a very powerful position.

Most parents realise exactly this and buy education at a particular school precisely for the positional advantages it conveys. Although the child is the beneficiary of the education, it is the parent who chooses and pays for it. The parent is the judge of the quality of what is on offer. But what of those children whose parents cannot afford such an education or who are not sufficiently knowledgeable to make a good choice? They will clearly be disadvantaged. It looks as if a market system of education is designed to favour the rich, knowledgeable and powerful. It is not a trade in commodities but a way of purchasing an advantageous upbringing. The supplier, particularly of prestigious education, is in a powerful position.

For this reason, more moderate advocates of markets in education do not recommend a completely unregulated and unsubsidised system such as the one we have just examined. It is much more common to hear proposals for regulated markets. One obvious problem is that of payment. If poor parents cannot pay for their children's education, then in a market system they will not get an education. Even if they are subsidised, their children will not get as good an education as those of rich parents. For this reason, it is common to hear of proposals for *vouchers* for education. A voucher is an educational entitlement with a certain cash value which is paid from general taxation. Vouchers are issued to parents for each child. It is up to parents to add their own money to the value of the voucher to purchase additional or higher quality education if they so wish. This proposal takes care of the objection that poor parents won't be able to afford education for their children, but it still leaves it vulnerable to the charge that vouchers favour the children of rich parents. In a state-funded education system, state education is paid for by taxation. Anyone who wishes to educate their child privately still has to pay a full contribution to state education. Under a voucher system they would not have this additional burden and many more reasonably well-off people would be able to buy extra education for their children than would be possible in a state-financed system.

Compulsory education

When education is provided by the state, it is usually compulsory. All taxpayers are compelled to pay and all parents are compelled to send their children to school. Some advocates of the market think that it is an infringement of parental rights to compel parents to send their children to school or to provide an education that is satisfactory to the state. They take the view that parents will realise that education is in the interests of children and will seek to provide the best that they can for them within the means that they have available. We have already seen in Chapter 8 the problems involved in ensuring that all workers receive training. We noted that for an individual firm it makes more sense not to train workers than to train them, unless there is some other reason, such as being taxed to provide training, which makes it make sense for them to train. Is there a parallel with the education of children?

A first point to bear in mind is that it is *children* who are to be educated not *parents*. Although everyone benefits from an educated population, through the skills and economic prosperity that they bring, all parents who pay for their children's education have to pay very high costs, with only a negligible addition to their own well-being as a result. Of course, they might pay for their child's education out of love or a sense of duty, but there are enough irresponsible parents around for it to be unrealistic to rely on the good sense of all parents to ensure that their children are educated. It is thus far from clear that parents would ensure that their children are educated. This is why even liberal commentators such as John Stuart Mill and Adam Smith have advocated a degree of compulsion to ensure that children are educated, even if the education system itself is run privately. In a market-led education system without compulsion, there are grounds for thinking that some parents would fail to educate their children. The issue is very similar to the training problem that we looked at in the previous chapter. When faced with the choice of whether to educate or not to educate in a private system, the 'educate' choice always involves an obvious and substantial parental cost, while the 'don't educate' choice does not.

If a parent chooses 'don't educate', if other parents educate, then they will benefit from the economic returns of living in a society with an educated population. On the other hand, if other parents don't educate, they will at least not lose out through paying for something that would be of little worth to them if they did it alone. This is because educational benefits are cumulative for the society. A society only obtains the benefits of education if there is a 'critical mass' of educated people. On the other hand, if they were to educate while everyone else did not, then they would incur a great deal of expenditure and very little gain. The rational choice would, therefore, be not to educate. It is common for the advocates for markets in education to argue that parents would feel a moral obligation to educate, irrespective of these calculating considerations. But markets work through the rational calculation of advantage, not through sentiment and moral obligation. So it is perverse for an advocate of markets to rely on moral obligation to make them work. It is no reply to say that one would still acquire the positional benefits of education, for these would accrue to the child educated, not to the parent paying for the education.

In a voucher system, education is compulsory and partially funded by taxation. Everyone would be taxed and part of the proceeds would go towards the cost of educational vouchers, which would be issued to all parents. Vouchers would ensure *adequate* educational opportunities for all. However, anyone who, as a committed parent, wished to spend more money on securing a school with smaller classes, better equipment or greater positional advantage for their child would be quite entitled to do so. In practice, some children would get much better educational opportunities than others, because of the ability of their parents to pay for better education.

Should we be happy with this? There are some good reasons for thinking not. First, one could say that the market would have failed in the aim of its advocates to provide the best possible education for everyone. This is clear enough; the best education would be provided for those whose parents had the longest purses. Access to a good education would be partly regulated through academic ability, since the best schools would have an interest in gaining pupils who were academically promising as well as having rich parents. The more prestigious they are, the better their chances of getting children who were both clever and rich. A child who could benefit from an education, of whatever kind, would only be able to do so if their parents could pay for them to enjoy it. Not only does this seem unfair, but it is not difficult to see that it could also have undesirable social consequences. Each generation of well-educated children would become parents and would use their wealth to ensure that their children enjoyed the best education, and so on. It would be very difficult for children of poor parents to benefit from the best education, even if they had the ability to do so. Social stagnation would result in a few generations, while the educationally underprivileged would become resentful and disillusioned.

Redistribution and market-led education

Would it be possible to retain the advantages of markets and eliminate their obvious injustices? One way of doing so would be to ensure that wealth was redistributed so drastically that no parent could take advantage of his or her purchasing power. Selection could then take place purely on the basis of the merits of the school and those of the children. This, however, looks like a desperate remedy to save market-based education. Whatever one thinks of the equal distribution of wealth, achieving educational fairness through this route is highly unlikely since it would prove to be highly unpopular politically. Even if it could be achieved, then it would not solve the problem of fair access. Even if all parents had the same income, it would still be open to them to dispose of it as they saw fit. Some might decide to spend more of their income on their children's education than others. They could still, therefore, buy educational privilege. Admittedly, the privilege would not now be so great because of the equalisation of incomes, but it would still be unfair.

There are more radical ways of reconciling the market with equal educational opportunity. Brighouse (2000b) has suggested, for example, that private schools should be prevented from selecting pupils according to their ability. Thus, although wealthy parents might pay more for educating their children privately, they would not be able to boost the opportunities of academically able children by allowing them to be educated *both* with other academically able children *and* in the best conditions that money could buy. The increased redistribution of wealth suggested above could be used, in turn, to boost the resources available to schools within the state sector. Allowing a degree of selection in state schools, while at the same time providing a high level of resources to schools for the pupils of the less able would further cut away at the advantages of the private schools and ensure that the least able children obtained a reasonable education.

Many of those who advocate markets in education would be horrified by these proposals. Most marketeers are opposed to redistribution and interference in the workings of the private sector of the economy. They also tend to be res-olutely opposed to interference in the ability of individuals to exercise free choice as to how they educate their children. However, many find market solu-tions repellent precisely because they seem to lead to very large inequalities within society. Indeed, it is difficult for those who advocate free markets in edu-cation to claim that they provide equal educational opportunities. Although all parents formally are allowed to send their children to private schools, few have the resources to actually do so. This means that, in practice, most children do not have any meaningful opportunity to enjoy the same educational privileges as the children of rich parents. But, as Brighouse has pointed out, there are ways, short of imposing complete equality of wealth, of providing many more equal opportunities within a market-based system. The most, it seems, that the fundamentalist free marketeer is prepared to allow is that the state should provide sufficient funding for the children of poor parents to obtain a decent minimum education. This is what Tooley (1998) refers to as *adequate* educa-tional opportunity. Of course, much turns here on what is meant by 'decent' and 'adequate'. In all such societies the children of the great majority of the population would be educationally disadvantaged relative to the children of the wealthy. The likely consequence would be that the society would develop a self-perpetuating elite who were able to transmit their privileges to the next genera-tion. Some would see it as a particularly odious system because of the apparent self-righteousness of those who benefit from it. The well-educated wealthy would be able to say to those who resented their position: 'Why do you com-plain, we achieved our positions through intelligence and hard work. Our ability benefits all of you as well as us. In seeking to change the education system you want to reward mediocrity and laziness.' As we have seen, this smug dismissal of the claims of others could hardly be justified. In effect, educational privilege and achievement would, to a large degree, have been bought in such a system.

Diversity in educational need: can the market provide?

Nevertheless we should not dismiss markets in education immediately because an extreme market solution produces unpleasant results. Pro-marketeers maintain that educational markets provide choice. Can those who advocate a state monopoly of education say the same? Let us suppose that we can blunt the criticism that educational markets promote inequality in the following way. As Brighouse suggests, incomes are substantially redistributed, private schools are not given a favourable tax regime and they are not allowed to select children by academic ability. Parents still have the choice of which school they send their children to, subject to availability of places. We might go further and suppose that no school is able to select by academic ability. How would such a system work?

The choice available in the system would be that different schools would cater to different *interests*, rather than to academic ability. By 'academic ability' is meant here, ability in writing, mathematics, science and history. Children's interests *might* be mainly in academic subjects, but they need not be. Some children may be interested in dance, others in music, some in sport, some in a business career, others in engineering, and so on. So a system of interviews and tests of interest could be used to screen children for different kinds of schools. In this way, diverse interests would be catered for and society would benefit from the variety of talents that were cultivated. If one were to take this proposal seriously, the investments needed to set up, say, a music specialist school, an engineering school or a business school would have to be considerable. Such schools need special buildings, special equipment and, ideally, teachers who have worked professionally in the specialist field. So they could not be a second-rate option, available only for children who failed to 'make the grade' academically, but they would be a highly attractive educational option in their own right. Children who attended such schools would be provided with very extensive resources and specialist teachers and would follow a course of study that would equip them for a well-paid and interesting career. The argument that markets only promote inequality and favour the rich and academically able would no longer be valid. Instead, markets would promote diversity and would provide particularly attractive options to children from backgrounds that typically did not value and cultivate academic achievement.

This looks like an attractive proposal to some equality-minded people. Let us consider the arguments against it first. One often-voiced objection is that children will be discouraged from pursuing an academic course of study. Second, and closely related to this, it will reinforce class divisions through segregating children into academic 'sheep' and practical 'goats'. Third, the practical option will always be looked down on by society. Finally, in a democracy only those with a good academic education will be able to participate in the governance of the society. None of these objections should be lightly dismissed. In particular, markets will respond to the wishes of consumers. If parents do not want a certain kind of education, then the market will not provide it. On the other hand, if there is inadequate educational choice, we will never know what parents would choose if a better choice were available. This brings us to the first objection, that children will be discouraged from pursuing an academic course. Many would say that, at present, children have little choice but to pursue an academic course, with few alternatives available. If markets work by making choices possible, schools that offer vocational routes will only flourish if parents want to send their children to them. The interesting question is, would they? As the position stands in the UK at the moment, with relatively little choice, we have no way of answering this question.

The 'academic sheep'/'non-academic goats' argument depends on an assumption that non-academic, vocationally oriented forms of study are intrinsically of less value than academic courses of study. We hope that enough has been said in Chapter 8 to dismiss this claim. We also saw in that chapter, that it is important that the choice is made at an appropriate time, not before the age of 14. This ensures that all children have a sufficient general education to become knowledgeable and potentially active citizens. Nor does a vocational education post-14 exclude the possibility of further civic and general education, as we saw in the previous chapter. Now it may be that vocational routes have a lower level of absolute esteem than academic ones. The critical question for policy-makers interested in offering choice at the middle and upper secondary levels, however, is whether or not such routes hold *enough esteem* for those who do not want to or find it difficult to pursue an academic route. There is a great deal of difference between someone holding a school in contempt and that person recognising that it is not the choice most highly regarded by society but is nevertheless the right choice for oneself. This point raises the third objection. Why should someone choose a lower prestige route?

Here we come to an interesting question. One feature of academic education is that relatively little in the way of specialist buildings and equipment is needed. This is not true of vocational and especially technical education, however. For example, a school which offered prevocational courses in engineering would need specialist buildings of appropriate structural strength, not to mention expensive equipment. Ideally such a school would be staffed by teachers with a real appreciation of the conditions in the engineering industry. Such an option would not come cheap. The kind of specialist school now being developed in the UK does not, for the most part, provide anything like this degree of provision for specialist forms of study. A key point is that *prestige* is partly determined by positional advantage (which vocational schools are not likely to have) and partly by the amount of money spent on provision. Since, proportionally the parents who are most likely to want to send their children to vocational schools are from the lower levels of socio-economic background (i.e. they are likely to be relatively poor), providing such schools is likely to involve redistribution, which many educational marketeers strongly dislike.

The need for accountability. Can the market provide this? Are parents good judges of educational offers?

One of the complaints levelled against state-run education is that it gives poor value for money in the sense that it is not responsive to the wants of the taxpaying public. Adam Smith's view that schoolmasters should not be wholly funded by the state 'lest they learn to neglect their business' is based on the view that people will act out of self-interest and, as such, they are interested in working as little as possible for as much as possible. If there is a guaranteed income from the state, teachers will not work as hard as they should. On the other hand, in a market system, they will only keep pupils if they teach them effectively. Their livelihoods will depend on satisfying the customer and hence they must be made to work in the customers' interests, not in their own. One does not need to make the cynical assumption that we only operate according to a narrow view of our own self-interest in order to see the force of the point about accountability. None of us are perfect. If there is never any check on what we do, we may become a little bit lazy, a little bit complacent and maybe a little bit arrogant, even with the best will in the world. So any system that wants to ensure that it is efficient and dedicated to its aims will need to pay attention to how it does what it says it will do.

This brings us straight to an important point. Who is the customer of education? To simplify the question, let us assume that the state, businesses, etc. are the go-betweens for the 'real' customers: parents and their children. But this leaves us with a problem, is it the parents or the child who should determine whether educators are doing what they are supposed to be doing? The parents, after all, pay for education, the child only 'consumes' it. On the other hand, since the parents don't go to school, how are they to tell whether they are getting 'value for money'? We have already seen that education can be seen as a 'prisoner's dilemma' in which the rational decision of a parent is not to educate. As we have seen, marketeers argue that they will feel a moral obligation to support their child through education. This is a little curious, since we are also told by the same marketeers that teachers cannot be trusted not to pursue their own interests to the detriment of their pupils. Why should it be any different with parents? And if parents do feel a moral obligation to fund their children's education, why should not teachers feel a moral obligation to teach them? So we need to be sure that parents will choose the option that is best for their child, not just the cheapest one.

But even if we can overcome this difficulty, there is another. We saw right at the beginning of this chapter that one needs to have product knowledge in order to make a rational market choice. We also saw that parents don't go to school. So how will they have appropriate knowledge of whether or not a school is working effectively? Pro-marketeers do not always make this easy for themselves in terms of the answers that they give. Those who are committed to the view that the aim of education is to provide educational opportunities are logically committed to the view that the way in which to assess the quality of educational provision is to see whether or not the opportunities are provided:

> Parents, for example, can ask children how they got on at school today, or why they are crying when they come home, or whether they have home-

work, and if not, why not. They can see the appearance of the students at the school, gauge the noise from the playground, and a multiplicity of other such factors.

(Tooley 1998, p. 273)

We have already commented on the wrongness of the idea that the aim of educational institutions is to provide educational opportunities rather than education. But let us, for a moment, concede this point. Could one assess the opportunities that a child has been offered using the techniques suggested? Without being unduly cynical, it seems naïve. Children can 'turn on the waterworks' to excite sympathy and divert attention from their own misdeeds. They are perfectly capable, like adults, of distorting the truth about what actually happened at school. Most teachers will be able to tell stories about how lazy children successfully conceal from their parents the amount of homework that they have to do. Finally, children are notoriously uncommunicative about what they have done at school. The appearance of pupils and the noise in the playground provide little or no information about the teaching and learning that go on in the classroom. As we have already seen, some market advocates reject assessment as a means of making schools accountable. Since their proposed instruments of accountability are clearly inadequate, we conclude that they have nothing useful to say about this matter.

This relates directly to a point made earlier on about the effective functioning of markets, namely the availability of *adequate knowledge* about offers in the marketplace. An educational specialist such as a teacher might be in a good position to make an informed assessment about how good a school is, but most parents don't have access to this expertise. Is there a way of providing the non-specialist with accurate information about the quality of schools? In Chapter 5 we argued at some length that there was. We can derive two sorts of information about academic achievement at schools. First, *output information* or a measure of attainment at the end of some educational process. Second, *progression information* or a measure of how far a pupil has progressed. As we argued in Chapter 5, strictly speaking, it is the latter measure, suitably contextualised, that provides us with an accurate picture of the effectiveness of the school.

However, as we also noted, there is too much of a margin of error in progression measurements to make meaningful comparison with any other than schools at the extremes of the performance range. Furthermore, from the point of view of education as a *positional* good, parents are interested in high absolute exit performance, rather than progress. It is the value of exit qualifications that counts on the credentials market, not progress *within* school, however successful. This means that, other things being equal, although schools that help their pupils to progress will be more popular than those that do not, most popularity will come from high exit performance. This in turn means that if assessment is used to construct league tables of school performance as a means of giving market information, then such a system of free choice will lead to competition for scarce places at the schools that achieve the best results for school-leaving certificates such as A levels in the UK. These exit results will not just depend on how good the progression achieved in the school was, but on how high the pupils were already achieving before they arrived at the school and on the academic ability of the children. Such schools will wish to recruit children who have already achieved high levels of performance and who have demonstrable academic ability. So a system of free choice will be one that selects according to academic ability.

This brings us finally to another issue that was originally raised by David Cooper (1980). Do we want our schools to allow some pupils to achieve the highest possible outcomes or do we wish for the highest possible overall level of achievement? A state system has some choice over what it wants as an educational aim. In some circumstances choosing a high overall level of achievement may mean putting considerable resources into the less academically able in order, for example, to develop their practical abilities. Such a strategy will only be possible in a market system that commits money to such schools, which tend to be quite expensive. We have already seen that this is possible, but that it might also involve a considerable degree of economic redistribution. However, to provide level funding to all schools and to allow the highest achievers to gravitate to those schools that have the highest exit achievements, will be to create a hierarchy with some very low-achieving schools at the bottom of the heap.

Conclusion

Educational markets are possible. Perceived achievement in public examinations will be the great driver of popularity, which will allow some schools to choose the pupils they want. There is some evidence that even within the state system, the ability to select will tend to increase educational inequality (Foster 2002). Moves to a voucher system will be tantamount to an educational subsidy to the wealthy. Since the children of the wealthy tend to achieve, on average, better results than the children of the less well-off, one would expect to find an even greater concentration of educational achievement among the wealthy than one does at the moment.

Of course, such a system will always allow a number of academically able poorer children to succeed, and wealthy schools can offer scholarships to poorer but able children. The real problem arises when one tries to reconcile such a system with *overall high levels of achievement*. Unless provision is made for good quality education for the less academically able, there are likely to be a large number of children with poor educational achievements. It will be difficult to develop a society in which skills are widely utilised and in which there are relatively small differences in wealth and income, while at the same time operating a market in education of whatever variety. Given that this is a question of justice as well as of advantage for society, it is quite rational to be concerned about such an outcome.

Questions for further discussion

1   Is it possible to reconcile equality and achievement within an education system?
2   What is wrong with believing that what an education system should offer is simply educational opportunities?
3   What place should parental choice have within an education system?
4   Who is the customer in the education system?
5   Is it possible for the educational 'customer' to gain enough knowledge of the educational opportunities on offer to make a rational choice?

Further reading

In recent years philosophers of education have paid considerable attention to markets and education. A useful introduction to the topic is *Education and the Market Place* (London, Falmer, 1994), edited by D. Bridges and T.H. McLaughlin. This book gives a range of views for and against the operation of markets in education. James Tooley is the philosopher of education most associated with the advocacy of educational markets. He has published three books on the subject, *Disestablishing the School* (Aldershot, Avebury, 1995), *Education without the State* (London, Institute of Economic Affairs, 1996) and *Reclaiming Education* (London, Cassell, 2000). He has engaged in lively polemic with his opponents in various journal articles (see below). Christopher Winch's *Quality and Education* (Oxford, Blackwell, 1996) contains a chapter critical of Tooley's view. This, in turn is replied to in Tooley's (1998) 'The "Neo-Liberal" Critique of State Intervention in Education: A Reply to Winch', *Journal of Philosophy of Education*, 32, 2: 107–121. A Reply by Winch, 'Markets, Equal Opportunities and Education: A Reply to Tooley' is to be found in the same journal, 32, 2: 429–436.

The redistributive market case for education is put by Harry Brighouse in his book *School Choice and Social Justice* (Oxford, Oxford University Press, 2000) and his Impact pamphlet *Educational Equality and the New Selective Schooling* (London, Philosophy of Education Society of Great Britain, 2000). Brighouse's position is criticised by Samara S. Foster (2002) in 'School Choice and Social Justice: A Response to Harry Brighouse', *Journal of Philosophy of Education*, 36, 2: 291–308.

Chapter 10

Education and multi-culturalism

In this chapter we address the issue of how an education system may accommodate diverse values and ways of life within a liberal democratic society. After surveying different broad approaches to this issue we relate our discussion to the previous ones concerning value diversity, citizenship and autonomy. We go on to look at some contemporary liberal responses to the issue and discuss communitarianism, or the view that the values of the particular community take priority over public values. Finally, as a case study, we take a detailed look at the debate concerning faith schools in the UK and show what a complex issue it is, before making our own suggestions as to its resolution. We choose faith schooling because it seems to exemplify the difficult issues that are involved, as well as being a question of contemporary relevance in more than one country.

Political and educational liberalism

It might be thought that a chapter concerned with multi-culturalism within education should focus upon ethnic diversity and the way in which such diversity may have an impact on education. However, a moment's reflection shows that the ethnic identity of a person or group has little to do with questions concerning education or educational policy. The issue is not about their ethnicity as such, but about the relationship of a person or group's culture and their values to the society in which they live and to the state to which they have allegiance. Broadly speaking, three kinds of approaches have been adopted to this question within modern educational systems. The first is known as 'assimilation'. This means that minority groups be encouraged or even pressurised into adopting the way of life of the host community.

The second is known as 'integration'. Integrationist approaches advocate that minority groups adhere to civic norms such as respect for the law, the political system, and economic relationships, but also adopt the language of the host community, at least outside the home context. Crucially, the integrationist maintains that children have a meaningful option to exit from the way of life enshrined in their own group when they reach maturity, should they so wish.

This means, in turn, that they are autonomous and that their education should prepare them to be autonomous (Burtonwood 2002). The third approach is sometimes called 'multi-cultural'. Multi-culturalists tend to be ambivalent concerning the question of whether minorities should adopt any of the practices and values of the host society. They tend to the view that communities have a right to preserve as much of their way of life as they see fit.

We will argue that some version of integration is the most desirable approach for liberal democracies. Ethnic communities are not to be asked to give up their way of life, but to make such accommodations to the host society so that that civil peace and, better, harmonious and productive relationships based on equality and mutual respect are promoted between all citizens. This, of course is an ideal that is easy to state and the way towards it is fraught with problems. Nevertheless, we believe that it is an ideal worth promoting and we discuss some of the central issues involved in trying to achieve it.

If the person or group shares the core values which underpin liberal democracy, and therefore an education within such a democracy, then there will be no theoretical problems for their integration within the mainstream culture. Even if there is a value divergence, for example, concerning food or mode of dress, this, insofar as such things are a matter of private choice, presents little problem for public policy within an integrationist perspective. It is only when such values are incompatible with, and therefore a challenge to, the values of other groups at the level of public policy that problems emerge. So, for instance, whether girls from an Islamic background choose to cover their heads in their private lives should not be a matter of public concern. However, if such a mode of dress in schools is thought to offend against the core values of the education system, for example, because such a system is essentially secular and certain forms of head cover are thought to flout this secularity, then this may become, as it has in France at the time of writing, a matter of public debate and, in the end, a matter of public policy. It is for this reason that education is at the heart of one of the central problems of liberal democracy. A liberal democracy, by its very nature, enshrines the values of political liberty and equality. But it does so, at least in large part, because it is aware of serving a community of diverse and sometimes competing interest groups who may not, or do not, endorse such values. Such groups may be based upon ethnicity but equally well may not, for example, the values of the British National Party, a far-right political party in the UK, are just as much a challenge to liberal democracy as fundamentalist Islam.

Such interest groups give rise to, accommodate and nurture ideals of the good life. These ideals may be self-directed – this is what we want for us and we want no one to impede us in its pursuit – but they may be, and often are, other-directed – this is what we want for everyone and we are willing to persuade, cajole or force everyone to join us in their pursuit. Thus, the competition here may not merely be for the requisite recognition and the resources and prestige that follow such recognition. Not merely for their share of the total cake, but, rather, for positions of influence and control whereby the processes of cake-making and distribution are directed. Such ambitions are not necessarily the result of selfish motivation. All too often, it is altruism that urges such groups to aspire to control the lives of the population at large. They want us to share their ideals, not because this is good for them, but because this will be good for us.

The liberal state sees itself as standing at the centre of this complex of competing and conflicting ideologies and attempts to act as a neutral referee between the different groups that represent such ideologies. Apart from its commitment to liberty and equality it has – at least in its most austere classical form (what we have called its universalist form) – no doctrine of the good life of its own. If it were to espouse such an ideal, it would either become merely another bearer of ideology in competition with the others or it would unfairly favour one of those already in existence. However, such a state, for reasons we have given in discussing the National Curriculum, has to educate the children of the different interest groups which form its base. And this is the problem. First, because it is not all clear that the liberal principles that apply to adults also apply to their children. Second, because the neutrality which is supposed to be *the* characteristic of the liberal state fits ill with any adequate notion of education.

Liberalism considers people to be as sane and reasonable adults. It allows and respects their choices because they are taken to be such. But if this is so, then the position of children within liberalism becomes problematic. If such children are seen as simply the property of particular adults, e.g. their parents, or particular social groups, then it might be the case that the liberals' only concerns will be with what such adults did with such property. But we know of no adequate conception of childhood which assigns only this limited status to children. Typically, a child is taken to be the locus of value in and for itself and that where we take particular adults to be 'responsible' for such a child, this responsibility has to be cashed, at least in large part, in terms of the independent interests of the child in question. This is to say that children can become rational self-choosing adults and that we – and the 'we' includes everyone who might be involved – have a duty to ensure that progress towards such autonomy is not impeded. So, for example, if it is agreed that education is a precondition of reaching autonomy, then this education may have to be imposed despite the current wishes of the child and the wishes of those held to be naturally responsible for such a child. Presumably this is a consensus arrived at by some kind of political agreement which takes into account the views of all sectors of the society. And if this applies to education as such, it may also apply to the parts of education. So, for instance, an overarching liberalism may insist that we are committedly illiberal when it comes to, say, the teaching of maths and science where what is important is not choice but simply getting it right. But this may also extend to more contentious areas. If, for example, we think that rational choice with regard to sexual matters has, as one of its conditions, an education in such matters, then this would be a very strong argument for giving children such an education. Thus, any liberal education of children may offend against the predilections of some of the groups whose children are being educated.

The above points are driven by the notion of children as unformed, trainee choosers. But they are buttressed by the nature of education itself. All conceptions of education are essentially normative. They necessarily involve a mixture of values and facts. Our conception of the content of education as detailed in our discussion of the curriculum embodies significant cultural values and also the value of critical enquiry. We envisage a situation in which children are both exposed to the best of the society's culture as that 'best' is chosen by a democratic consensus, and where they are taught to critically reflect upon that culture. Both of these value commitments may also offend some of the constituent groups within the state. The first, because it will try to show a range of things on offer, not all of which might be approved of by any constituent group. The second, because critical reflection, in the jargon of today, tends to be a transferable skill which, if it can be applied to the cultural goodies on offer, can also be applied to the position on culture which is taken by the child's parent group.

So, the nature of children and the nature of education both push us towards educational policies which go beyond mere cultural reproduction. There is a chance that the recipients of such policies will end up rejecting at least some of what they have been offered either within the ambit of their education or from their own cultural groups. Education can be profoundly subversive of any given status quo. It may lead people to reject their cultural backgrounds and thereby put the continued existence of such backgrounds at risk. But, if a liberal education is subversive in the sense that it nurtures the challenge to old certainties, in another sense it will aim at social reproduction. Illiberal cultural and political groups acquiesce to liberalism as a matter of accidental political expediency, but the liberal compromise will not sustain itself unless some, at least, positively endorse its values. A liberal education therefore will at least contain the hope that some being educated will come to see such an education, not as a necessary expedient in the present situation, but as a good thing in and for itself.

Let us put some of the above points into the context of current liberal debate. John Rawls is *the* great modern political philosopher. His book, *A Theory of Justice* (1971) breathed life into an almost moribund philosophical discipline, and at the same time, presented its readers with a thorough, inventive and passionate defence of modern liberalism. Over the past thirty odd years he has defended and refined his original views and his *Political Liberalism* (1993) gives his later views on many of the topics covered by the earlier book. Rawls' achievements are beyond question. A continuing theme of his work is a minimalist notion of political liberalism which stresses the impartiality of the state with regard to conceptions of the good life, and which is consistently concerned that the values inherent within liberalism – values associated with autonomy and individuality – do not become just 'another sectarian doctrine' (Rawls

1985, p. 246). To this end he rejects a fully blown liberalism which promotes such values and defends instead a much weaker version, which requires of education not an espousal of such values but:

> Far less. It will ask that the children's education include such things as knowledge of their constitutional and civic rights so that, for example, they know that liberty of conscience exists in their society and that apostasy is not a legal crime, all this to ensure that their continued membership when they come of age is not based simply on ignorance of their basic rights or fear of punishment for offences that do not exist. Moreover, their education should also prepare them to be fully cooperating members of society and enable them to be self-supporting; it should also encourage the political virtues so that they want to honour the fair terms of social cooperation in their relations with the rest of society.
>
> (1993, pp. 199–200)

If we look at the second sentence here its requirements could, perhaps, be satisfied by a notice on the school noticeboard which outlined the children's basic legal rights (much in the way that factories in England used to display copies of Factory Acts on their noticeboards). However, no sensible person could think this is sufficient for giving children a real experience of the possibility of choice. The awareness that Rawls talks of here may be one of the conditions for a reasonable education but it could only fulfil this role if embodied in educational processes which stressed an active commitment to autonomy. The second part of the passage is much more ambiguous and, on some possible readings, sits ill with the first part. So, for instance, if we take his talk of encouraging the political virtues seriously so that children 'want to honour the fair terms of social cooperation', this looks much more like an education which is fully engaged with the promotion of liberal virtues. An education which seeks, as we mentioned above, to produce people who value liberalism rather than simply tolerate it.

This uncertainty with regard to state action, e.g. through education, infects even those who are prepared, unlike Rawls, to argue for a comprehensive, active liberalism. So, for instance, Thomas Nagel in *Equality and Partiality* says at one point, concerning education: 'A society should try to foster the creation and preservation of what is best, or as good as it possibly can be, and this is just as important as the widespread dissemination of what is just good enough' (1991, p. 135) which echoes what we have been saying. However, later in the same book he writes:

> the role of the state as an actor on behalf of its citizens assumes prominence when the action is based on commitment to values in direct contradiction to the deepest convictions of some citizens about the meaning of life. That, I think, is deeply offensive and unacceptable, and forfeits the state's claim

to represent them in a way in which the promotion of other values some of them do not share does not.

(ibid., p. 167)

In the context of a discussion of education – which is not Nagel's context at this point – such a position ignores two essential points. First, education cannot, even in the full-blown critical version that we are offering, contradict in any serious way the 'deepest convictions ... about the meaning of life' of those being educated. For education, in our sense, is a preparation for making choices about such a meaning and it therefore presupposes that those being educated have not, as yet, rationally chosen in this area. Second, there can be absolutely no guarantee that the fully formed convictions of the parents of those being educated, and their cultural group generally, will not include a version of the meaning of life which either precludes their children being educated at all; or precludes the type of education that we are advocating; or precludes facets of that education, e.g. its commitment to gender equality. And such people, we suspect, will not be mollified by being told that such an education is not for *them* but for children, who are not simply to be seen as replacements for them.

In such a situation the liberal state can either retreat to one version of the Rawlsian position, where no serious liberal education is on offer, or, and this is our preferred alternative, it can insist that all its children in state-funded schools are given a liberal education despite the outrage this causes some of their parents.

Nagel's uneasiness on this point is shown earlier in the same chapter when he does mention education:

> The true liberal position ... is committed to refusing the power of the state to impose paternalistically on its citizens a good life individualistically conceived ...
>
> The consequences of this position are complex, for there are several ways in which state action may serve a conception of the good, and they will not all be equally unacceptable to those who do not share it. (1) A state might force people to live in accordance with that conception, or prohibit them from living in ways it condemns. (2) A state might support the realisation of the preferred conception, be it education or resource allocation, thus involving all citizens and taxpayers indirectly in its service. (3) A state might adopt policies for other reasons which have the effect of making it easier for one conception to be realised than another, thus leading to growth in adherence to the one as opposed to the other.
>
> Clearly the first way is the most illegitimate; examples are restrictions on free exercise of religion, on the basic style of personal life, or on private sexual conduct. The second is less of an assault on individuals who do not share the dominant values, but still of questionable legitimacy; the clearest example would be the public support of an established church. The third is

in some degree unavoidable; liberal toleration, for example, though not motivated by the aim of promoting secularism and discouraging religious orthodoxy, may have these effects, nonetheless.

(ibid., pp. 165–166)

The key category here is (2). Nagel seems to miss the point that his talk of education under this category can be interpreted in at least two ways and while one of these fits with his defining example, the other does not. So, he is right to hold that state support for an established church may be offensive to citizens who are not within that church. And state support for education which prepared people for membership of such a church would be equally offensive. (The situation in England, where the blasphemy laws only apply to Christianity, also offends against liberalism. But the obvious liberal solution here is *not* to extend such laws to all religions but rather to have no blasphemy laws.) But the type of liberal education that we are supporting, with its critical emphasis, is diametrically opposed to such a preparation. It is certainly paternalistic, but then how could it not be, given that it is designed for children who, as yet, have not a full conception of their own good? – but it aims to enable the people being educated not simply to fit in with this or that church, or no church at all, but rather to choose rationally – insofar as this is possible – between any of the various faiths on offer, or at least to be able to rationally defend *post hoc* their particular commitments. It may be the case, as Nagel notes with category (3), that such an educational policy, in implying that all such faiths are of equal intellectual standing, has the effect of encouraging agnosticism at the very least. But this, we think, is one of the unavoidable consequences of a thought-through policy of liberal education.

Such a conception of education cannot, of course, require that those being educated retain its critical spirit after the completion of their education. A relapse into the unexamined life must always be a real possibility. But, to the extent that it impinges on learners, it is likely to be subversive of many modes of social life and thus cut people somewhat adrift from their social moorings. Its impartiality over matters, that may not be rationally decidable, will not necessarily extend to all those areas of the curriculum where some interest groups would claim undecidability. Thus, despite the fact that there still are Flat Earth Societies, this does not mean that the views of such societies are entitled to an equal place on the curriculum with more enlightened views of the Earth. Here, if not elsewhere, there are arguments which decide the matter. The same is true, as we have said elsewhere, with creationist opposition to evolution. Again, rational scientific argument gives us a preferred option to teach. The fact, if it is a fact, that some people believe in fairies gives us no reason *in itself* for presenting fairy lore to children in our schools.

Liberty

The disagreements within liberalism outlined above, and the place of education within such disagreements, can also be placed within the long-running debate concerning negative and positive liberty. The terms and key distinctions of this important debate were introduced in Isaiah Berlin's (1969) paper, 'Two Concepts of Liberty'. There Berlin distinguishes between *negative* liberty which is, roughly, the freedom from the coercion of others in an agent's actions and *positive* liberty which, again roughly, consists of self-mastery. So, for instance, according to Berlin, I can legitimately claim to lack freedom if others interfere in my attempted realisation of my own plans and projects but I cannot legitimately make such a claim because I am not able to fly like a bird. This latter lack of capacity has nothing to do with, and is dangerously conflated with, real political freedom. This means that if I am stupid, ill-informed, lacking in resolution, I may regret my state but I cannot, properly, lament over a lack of liberty or freedom.

For Berlin, only negative liberty is worth pursuing as a political good. The pursuit of positive liberty by a political regime, the attempt by such a regime to correct people's regrettable false consciousness and therefore their lack of identification with, for instance, their true class destiny or the true goals of the General Will,[1] as, of course, clearly discerned by the regime itself, leads gradually, but inexorably, towards totalitarian tyranny. In seeking to control, rather than respond to, the wishes of the people, such a regime leaves all real freedom far behind.

There is much that is importantly true about such an analysis. However, as with Rawls' account, the distinction it draws is too stark. It assumes, as he does, that polities are made up of autonomous choosers who have sprung fully formed into the world like Athena from the head of Zeus. It therefore never asks whether politics has a place in producing such choosers. In other words, it almost completely neglects the role of education within our society. But, in neglecting this, it neglects some of the dimensions of political freedom. There are at least some aspects of self-mastery which any respectable liberal theorist must address. In any society in which some people are left stupid or ignorant because of their lack of a proper education, *and this lack could be addressed by other people within that society*, we can, we think, perfectly legitimately talk about such a group lacking political freedom. If, as J.S. Mill argues in On Liberty the 'distinctive endowment of a human being' are 'the human faculties of perception, judgement, discriminative feeling, mental activity, and even moral preference' and if these 'are exercised only in making a choice' ([1859] 1968, p. 116) then any political arrangement that neglects, either deliberately or through inadvertence, to train and nurture such faculties through education, can be accused of acting against the freedom of at least some of its people. This is the point of an education for autonomy, we assume that possession of autonomy is necessary for a worthwhile life in societies like ours, and we prepare children to exercise it in their adult lives.

Communitarianism

So far in this chapter, we have examined the place of education within contemporary theories of liberal democracy and argued that such theories need to be rather more capacious than they normally are to accommodate an adequate version of liberal education. For some of the critics of liberalism, the advocacy of freedom, autonomy and quality make it philosophically and politically incoherent. Communitarians, such as MacIntyre, Taylor and Sandel, think that liberalism conceives of people as isolated individuals who, within their own sphere, discern and pursue their own good in their own way. Although they may pick and choose between the customs, traditions, conventions and cultural items on offer within their own societies, such choice, in itself, implies no prior attachment to any of the things chosen between. The liberal autonomous chooser *creates* their good out of what is on offer but comes unencumbered and clear sighted to such a choice. Such a picture, according to the communitarians, simply does not make sense. People are not free-floating choosers of value, rather, their very identity is constituted by the communities in which they are born and brought up and thus their understanding of values and choices is embedded within the institutional frameworks of such communities and the virtues and dispositions which are inculcated in its members. People cannot disengage from their communities without a serious loss of self. Given that what they are is partly constituted by the cultural norms of their communities what choices they can see as open, or not open, to them will also be determined by such norms. If such criticism of liberalism is sound, then it must also threaten our version of liberal education, for that, like its parent political theory, lays stress upon autonomy and the creation of value by self commitment.

But are such criticisms sound? Before approaching this question directly it is salutary to dwell for a moment on the societal and educational implications of an extreme version of communitarian doctrines. Such implications are overwhelmingly and unappealing conservative. If all that a society, and the educational systems within such a society, can do is to accept the communities within that society as they are, and therefore to accept as given values of individuals within such communities, then the most that any society can hope for is the continued existence of the status quo. It is either this or anarchy. But what this might mean in practice is that if such communities embody, as they very well might, deeply entrenched sexist or racist values, we may, as a kind of holding operation, enact legislation to prevent the implementation of such values within the wider society, but we can have no reasonable hope of touching the values themselves! Even such legislation will, to the members of such a community, seem like merely the imposition of the alien norms of the dominant power within such a society. But it also follows, if communitarians are right, that, as education is by its nature normative, and as the only norms available exist within communities, that the only sensible education policy would be one in which such communities controlled the manner and matter of their own educational institutions. So, for instance, we might be faced not only by communities which exhibited values which might be abhorrent to the majority of people within the society, but with state-funded community schools which were deliberately designed to nurture such values.

But are the communitarian criticisms of liberalism sound? We think not for various reasons. First, communitarians tend to radically over-emphasise the homogeneity of the communities they describe and over-simplify the interaction of these communities and those that surround them. There may be communities, such as the Amish in America, which seem to speak with a single voice and where contact with surrounding communities is rare, but such communities – although they may pose special problems – are far from the norm in modern nation–states. Within all, even moderately complex, communities there will be varieties of opinion concerning values and such variety will be fostered by the everyday contact that the members of the community have with the 'outside' world and the massive communication potential of the modern world. Such variety of opinion within communities is often not fully appreciated. So, for example, when the Rushdie *Satanic Verses* affair was at its height, one of the writers of this book found himself at conference after conference explaining to Third World Muslim and non-Muslim critics of Rushdie that the author of the offending book was not one of us – from outside their culture – speaking to them, but rather one with important familial and cultural links with them – speaking to them.

Second, although it may be difficult for people to re-evaluate the values that one absorbs at one's parents' – and therefore their communities – knees, it is not, contrary to some communitarian thinking, e.g. Sandel (1998), impossible. Of course, one cannot question all of one's given values at the same time, nevertheless, it seems perfectly possible to question them one by one over time. And we know, from looking around us – or, perhaps, looking within ourselves – that even those values which seem to be fundamental can, perhaps with some effort, be changed. Catholics become atheists and vice versa, pacifists become soldiers, intellectuals become farmers, and the list of changes goes on and on. Such a point should be easy for a communitarian such as MacIntyre to grasp, given that he has been in turn an atheist, a Marxist and a Catholic.

Our contact with the world transforms us and often such transformation finds its heart in our education. We know of no communitarian theory of education but, should one come to exist, we can envisage no way in which it could accommodate this power of education to transform lives and thereby identities. One of the striking features of contemporary British higher education is the fact that a large number of its teachers, who, because of their jobs, are the purveyors of high culture, come from backgrounds which, at least in this sense of culture, were culturally impoverished. These people are the recipients of the largesse of the 1944 Education Act which made secondary schooling compulsory and are therefore the first generation in their families, and often some of the first in their communities, to receive a university education. Any liberal theory of education which ignores such people must be flawed and any theory of politics which denies the possibility of such people must be wrong. Autonomy implies the ability of people to rationally evaluate received values and outlook.

Our final criticism of communitarianism harks back to some points we made at the beginning of this chapter. Because communitarian thinking subordinates individuals to their cultural context, it runs the risk of making their cultural identities a matter of imperatives rather than of historical explanation, of telling people who they must be despite their explicit dissent. This is bad enough when such people are adults, because in being adults they can assess the risk of their own bloodymindedness, and, if things get too bad, go elsewhere. But such subordination when applied to children is, in fact, just as bad although often more insidious. It is to treat then simply as a means to cultural reproduction. The fact that as children they cannot consent or dissent from such a process does not excuse it. Of course, parents and the communities parents come from want their children to grow up and become certain types of adult. But any liberal system of education which does not take into account the possibility that the children will come not to share the dreams and hopes of the parents, threatens such children with great harm within a liberal society. It threatens to ignore their rights as people in favour of a dubious right of mechanical cultural reproduction. No cultural group has an absolute and divine right to continued existence. Such existence is a matter for the consenting adults within such groups. And this means that no cultural group can rightfully press-gang non-consenting adults and non-adults to further their particular cause.

Faith schools

Some of the themes dealt with above have resurfaced, albeit in a minor key, in a discussion about 'faith' schools in Britain. There are many such schools, largely Church of England, and each school is overwhelmingly funded by the state. In a society where there was one religious group and a large part of the population who were either indifferent to, or hostile concerning religion; the liberal case against faith schools would be simple. A democratic liberal state should, as far as is possible, be neutral towards competing conceptions of the good life. Such neutrality *might* allow such a state to tolerate faith schooling outside the state education system, but it cannot, without ceasing to be liberal, endorse such schooling within state-funded education. For a state to endorse either a religion as such or a particular religion is for it to offend against the notions of neutrality and justice which are, at least partially, constitutive of liberalism. In the light of this, the state religion of England and Wales and the selective blasphemy laws in place in our society are major offences against liberalism. The state funding of faith schools in the above imagined society would be on a par with such offences.

However, the case becomes much more complicated in a society which is largely secular, but in which there are significant minorities attached to differ-ent faiths e.g. Christianity, Judaism and Islam, where the state even-handedly offers to fund faith schools of all religious persuasions. Here – and we take this to be our particular situation – much turns on whether such an offer of funding must be seen as the state *endorsing* religion as such or particular religions. On the one hand, it could be claimed that the secular nature of most schools is, at least, an implicit endorsement by the state of a secular view of the good life and that in being open-handed towards all religions, the state is retaining the neu-trality needed for liberal credentials. On the other hand, it could be argued, that the secular nature of most schools is to be expected in a liberal society because this simply expresses the neutrality we expect in such a society and that there-fore, any offer of funding for faith schools, however even-handed, is a departure from such neutrality. Certainly the secular majority might find such funding offensive and, for the pupils in the faith schools, state funding might appear as an endorsement. It is also the case that faith schools might be taken as divisive and therefore should not receive funding in a liberal polity where one of the central purposes of the polity is to emphasise the things that help to hold the society together, rather than those things that might divide it. The authors of this book cannot agree as to which of the above arguments is sound. It might help a reader to make up their own mind if they consider what we take to be a parallel example. In any liberal society it would be wrong to fund any one of the political parties on offer. Would the wrongness disappear should the state offer to fund all viable political parties?

Whatever the answer to the above, it is clear that some of the defences of faith schools do not even begin to address the relevant questions. So, for instance, in this context, it would not do to argue that such schools serve their pupils well in public examinations. If it could be shown – and we do not think it can be – that such schools overwhelmingly outperform their non-religious equivalents, i.e. not just the non-religious, non-selective school that happens to be down the road from a particular high-performing religious school, but non-religious schools generally, then there might be a case, in terms of social utility, to defend such schools. But such a case would not, in itself, get rid of the liberal doubts raised above.

We have heard it urged, by the authors of an unpublished monograph on faith schools, McLaughlin and Halstead, that there is no logical reason why the curriculum within faith schools and the teachers who deliver such a curriculum cannot meet the tests of neutrality demanded by our notion of liberal educa-tion. And it is certainly the case that this is not logically impossible. However, this logical possibility does not silence several points that seem extremely perti-nent to the argument. First, why should the state entrust such neutrality to institutions or people within institutions who are not, by their very nature, generally neutral? There is no doubt, for instance, that it is logically possible for a known Tottenham Hotspur player, say, a member of the first team who happens to be suffering from a minor injury, to neutrally referee their next game against Arsenal. But no Arsenal supporter or impartial member of the public would be happy with such a situation. Second, if the manner and matter of education within faith schools are to be neutral in the way in which McLaughlin and Halstead suggest, then what is the point of faith schools from the point of view of the faith concerned? Either such schools do nothing to promote a particular faith, in which case there seems little reason for that faith to offer them financial support, or they do something, in which case they offend against liberal neutrality. If the answer to this is that the churches simply, from motives of pure charity, wish to involve themselves in the good that education can do, then it can be suggested that such involvement can take place without there being faith schools.

One of the most percipient commentators on liberalism and its critics has been Will Kymlicka (1995a). It is therefore good to see his work used in the faith schools debate even if, as we shall argue, the implications of such work are misunderstood. In 'Why Should States Fund Denominational Schools?' (de Jong and Snick 2002) try to show, using Kymlicka, that a compromise is possible between the supporters of faith schools and their critics. For this they use Kymlicka's point that cultural membership has a place with liberty among the primary goods that should be respected in a liberal society. Such primary goods express values that should be accepted by any member of such a society despite their different conceptions of the good life. Secondary goods are those that are derived from these different conceptions. According to de Jong and Snick, if we take cultural membership as a primary good along with autonomy, then we might fund primary schools which are expressive of the values of particular cultural groups, whereas our secondary schools would be devoted to the value of autonomy.

We can see why it might be thought that Kymlicka's suggestion does support such a compromise. However, we think such an interpretation is mistaken. Even if, as is claimed, cultural membership is a primary good, this does not mean that this must figure in the educational arrangements of a liberal state. Such a state must respect such membership and such respect implies that, all things being equal, it must not deny people the opportunity for such membership. So, for instance, it must not, as has happened in America and Australia in the past, try to suppress the language of cultural groups or remove the children of cultural groups so that they can be brought up among people of the dominant culture. Such practices offend against liberal notions of the neutral state in the same way that active support of particular groups would also offend. But, apart from duties of non-interference, little else follows. As communitarians have stressed, membership of a particular cultural group is a given, i.e. we are born and brought up within such a group, and as a given it does not stand in need of state support. The nurturing of autonomy, which we see as the aim of state education, must again, by its very nature, involve the possibility that the autonomous individual will choose to return to perhaps uncritical membership of such a group. No reasonable state can demand of its mature citizens that they eschew such membership. But again, this does not lead to any particular pattern of state funding for education.

There are points that Kymlicka (1995b, Chapter 7) makes concerning the importance of language in cultural formation which might imply that a state education system should, at least at some levels, make provision for mother tongue teaching. It also may be the case that in a multi-cultural and multi-lingual society we need to look carefully at what languages are on offer with second language teaching, e.g. might there not be a strong case for offering some of the languages from the Indian subcontinent to white children in Bradford and Leicester? But neither of these suggestions means that the state should, for the first six years of a child's school life, endorse the particular values of that child's cultural group.

We have argued that education must play a crucial role in any liberal society. So crucial that any suggestions for educational initiatives must always be approached with the utmost care and critical spirit. If the existence of a liberal society matters – and it does – then the place of education within such a society is of extreme importance.

Conclusion

We think that democratic liberalism is the only acceptable political theory for societies like ours in the Western world. Such a liberalism has its problems but such problems should not make us blind to the unacceptable nature of most of the alternatives on offer. One of the things that liberals must do if such liberal societies are to sustain themselves is to take seriously the role of education within such societies. If one makes this role too thin, as we have argued that Rawls does, then in a very short time, liberalism may collapse into one of the illiberal alternatives. However, if one makes it too thick, then we do have the problem of securing democratic consent. The need here is to *argue* for a satisfactory conception of education rather than assume that the task can be solved by stipulation.

Questions for discussion

1 Why is neutrality an essential component of liberal societies?
2 What is the difference between a liberal society tolerating illiberal views and endorsing them?
3 Make a case for or against faith schools.
4 Is communitarianism essentially conservative?
5 If a society does not educate its children, is it thereby harming them?

Further reading

Stephen Mulhall and Adam Swift's *Liberals and Communitarians* (Oxford, Blackwell, 1996) is a good introduction to contemporary liberal and communitarian thinking. Harvey Siegel's *Rationality Redeemed* (New York, Routledge, 1997) is a lively defence of a liberal view of education against critics from various perspectives. For an overview of the discussion within philosophy of education the symposium 'Five Critical Stances towards Liberal Philosophy of Education in Britain' initiated by John White, and with replies by Wilfred Carr, Richard Smith, Paul Standish and Terence McLaughlin gives an excellent snapshot of the debate at the moment, *Journal of Philosophy of Education*, 37, 1 (2003), with a full bibliography.

Notes

2 Culture and the curriculum

1 See Woodhead (1985) for a detailed survey of the long-term effects of these projects.
2 Much of this chapter is based upon a longer work cowritten by one of the authors which explores these issues in greater depth. See Gingell and Brandon (2000).
3 See Peters (1966) for such a characterisation, especially Part I.
4 This utilitarian function of education has not been given the prominence in the literature that we think it deserves. However, it has been admirably defended over the years by Robin Barrow. See Barrow (1976, 1981).
5 See R. Alexander (1992).

5 Standards, performance and assessment

1 Astonishingly, the National Curriculum bungles this point, stating that 'The school curriculum should aim to provide opportunities for all pupils to learn and to achieve' (DfEE 1999). This statement undercuts the concern with assessment that is so prominent in the policy of successive British governments.

10 Education and multi-culturalism

1 Rousseau's doctrine, in *The Social Contract* concerning the securing of agreement in his account of a democratic community. For a discussion, see Dent (1988).

Select bibliography

Ainley, Patrick and Rainbird, Helen (eds) (1999) *Apprenticeship: Towards a New Paradigm of Learning*, London, Kogan Page.

Alexander, Robin (1992) *Policy and Practice in the Primary School*, London, Routledge.

Archard, David (2000) *Sex Education*, London, PESGB.

Aristotle (1925) *The Nichomachean Ethics*, translated by David Ross, London, Dent.

Arnold, Matthew ([1869] 1935) *Culture and Anarchy*, J. Dover Wilson (ed.), Cambridge, Cambridge University Press.

Ashton, David and Green, Francis (1996) *Education, Training and the Global Economy*, Cheltenham, Edward Elgar.

Bantock, Geoffrey H. (1971) 'Towards a Theory of Popular Education', in R. Hooper (ed.), *The Curriculum: Context, Design and Development*, Edinburgh, Oliver and Boyd.

Barrow, Robin (1976) *Common Sense and the Curriculum*, Brighton, Harvester.

—— (1978) *Radical Education*, Oxford, Martin Robinson.

—— (1981) *The Philosophy of Schooling*, Brighton, Harvester.

—— (1984) *Giving Teaching Back to Teachers*, Brighton, Harvester.

—— (1987) 'Skill Talk', *Journal of Philosophy of Education*, 21, 2: 187–195.

—— (1993) *Language, Intelligence and Thought*, Aldershot, Edward Elgar.

Barrow, Robin and Woods, Ronald (1975) *Introduction to the Philosophy of Education*, London, Methuen.

Barry, Norman (1995) *An Introduction to Modern Political Theory*, 2nd edition, London, Methuen.

Berlin, Isaiah (1969) 'Two Concepts of Liberty', in I. Berlin, *Four Essays on Liberty*, Oxford, Oxford University Press.

Bernstein, Basil (1973) *Class, Codes and Control*, vol. 1, London, Paladin.

Best, David (1992) *The Rationality of Feeling*, Brighton, Falmer.

Bramall, Steve and White, John (2000) *Will the New National Curriculum Live up to its Aims?* London, Philosophy of Education Society of Great Britain.

Bridges, D. and McLaughlin, T.H. (1994) *Education and the Market Place*, London, Falmer.

Brighouse, Harry (2000a) *School Choice and Social Justice*, Oxford, Oxford University Press.

—— (2000b) *Educational Equality and the New Selective Schooling*, London, Philosophy of Education Society of Great Britain.

Brighouse, Harry (2002) 'A Modest Defence of School Choice', *Journal of Philosophy of Education*, 36, 2: 291–308.

Burt, Cyril (1949) 'The Structure of the Mind', in S. Wiseman (ed.), *Intelligence and Ability*, London, Penguin.

Burtonwood, Neil (2002) 'Political Philosophy and the Lessons for Faith-based Schools', *Educational Studies*, 28, 3: 239–252.

Callan, Eamonn (1993) *Autonomy and Schooling*, Kingston, Ontario, McGill Queen's University Press.

Carr, David (1980) 'Knowledge in Practice', *American Philosophical Quarterly*, 18, 1.

—— (1991) *Educating the Virtues*, London, Routledge.

—— (1999) 'Professional Education and Professional Ethics', *Journal of Applied Philosophy*, 16, 1: 33–46.

—— (2003) *Making Sense of Education*, London, Routledge.

Carr, David and Steutel, Jan (eds) (1999) *Virtue Ethics and Moral Education*, London, Routledge.

Clarke, Linda and Wall, Christine (2000) 'Craft Versus Industry: The Division of Labour in European Housing Construction, *Construction Management and Economics*, 18: 689–698.

Clarke, Linda and Winch, Christopher (2004) 'Apprenticeship and Applied Theoretical Knowledge', *Educational Philosophy and Theory*, 36, 5.

Cooper, D. (1980) *Illusions of Equality*, London, Routledge.

Crick, Bernard (1999) 'The Presuppositions of Citizenship Education', *Journal of Philosophy of Education*, 33, 3: 317–336.

Crouch, Colin; Finegold, David and Sako, Mari (1999) *Are Skills the Answer? The Political Economy of Skill Creation in Advanced Industrial Countries*, Oxford, Oxford University Press.

Davis, Andrew (1995) 'Criterion-Referenced Assessment and the Development of Knowledge and Understanding', *Journal of Philosophy of Education*, 29, 1: 3–22.

—— (1998) *The Limits of Educational Assessment*, Oxford, Blackwell.

—— (1999) *Educational Assessment: A Critique of Current Policy*, London, Philosophy of Education Society of Great Britain.

Davis, Andrew and White, John (2001) 'Accountability and School Inspection: In Defence of Audited Self-Review', *Journal of Philosophy of Education*, 35, 4: 667–682.

Dearden, Robert (1979) 'The Assessment of Learning', *British Journal of Educational Studies*, 27, 2: 111–124.

—— (1984) 'Education and Training', *Westminster Studies in Education*, 7: 57–66.

Dearden, Robert; Hirst, Paul and Peters, Richard S. (1970) *Education and the Development of Reason*, London, Routledge.

de Jong, Johan and Snick, Oer (2002) 'Why Should States Fund Denominational Schools?' *Journal of Philosophy of Education*, 36, 4: 573–587.

Dent, Nicholas (1988) *Rousseau*, Oxford, Blackwell.

DES (1988) *The National Curriculum*, London, HMSO.

Dewey, John (1933) *How We Think*, Chicago, Henry Regnevey.

DfEE (1999) *The National Curriculum*, London, HMSO.

Eliot, T.S. (1948) *Notes Towards a Definition of Culture*, London, Faber and Faber.

Entwistle, Harold (1970) *Education, Work and Leisure*, London, Routledge.

Eysenck, Hans (1973) *The Inequality of Man*, London, Collins.

Flew, Anthony (1976) *Sociology, Equality and Education*, London, Macmillan.

—— (2000) *Education for Citizenship*, London, Institute of Economic Affairs.

Galton, Francis [1892] *Hereditary Genius*, extracts in Stephen Wiseman (ed.) (1973) *Intelligence and Ability*, London, Penguin, pp. 25–36.

Gingell, John (1985) 'Art and Knowledge', *Educational Philosophy and Theory*, 17, 1: 10–21.

—— (2001) 'Against Creativity', *Irish Educational Studies*, 20: 25–37.

Gingell, John and Brandon, Edwin (2000) *In Defence of High Culture*, Oxford, Blackwell.

Gingell, John and Winch, Christopher (2000) 'Curiouser and Curiouser: Davis, White and Assessment', *Journal of Philosophy of Education*, 34, 4: 687–696.

Goldstein, Harvey (1995) *Interpreting International Comparisons of Student Achievement*, Paris, UNESCO.

Goldstein, Harvey; Huiqi, Pan; Rath, Terry and Hill, Nigel (2000) *The Use of Value Added Information in Judging School Performance*, London, Institute of Education.

Gordon, J.C.B. (1981) *Verbal Deficit*, London, Croom Helm.

Gray, John (1995) 'Agonistic Liberalism', in *Enlightenment's Wake*, London, Routledge.

Green, Andy (1990) 'Education and State Formation', London, Macmillan.

Green, Andy; Wolf, Alison and Leney, Tom (1999) *Convergence and Divergence in European Education and Training Systems*, London, Institute of Education.

Hager, Paul (2000) 'Know-how and Workplace Practical Judgment', *Journal of Philosophy of Education*, 34, 2: 281–296.

Hamlyn, David (1978) *Experience and the Growth of Understanding*, London, Routledge.

Haydon, Graham (1999) *Values, Virtues and Violence*, Oxford, Blackwell.

Herrnstein, R. (1996) *The Bell Curve*, London, New York, Free Press.

Hirst, Paul (1965a) 'Liberal Education and the Nature of Knowledge', in R. Archambault (ed.), *Philosophical Analysis and Education*, London, Routledge.

—— (1965b) 'Morals, Religion and the Maintained School', *British Journal of Educational Studies*, 14: 5–18.

—— (1973) 'What is Teaching?', in R.S. Peters (ed.), *The Philosophy of Education*, Oxford, Oxford University Press.

—— (1974) *Knowledge and the Curriculum*, London, Routledge.

—— (1993) 'Education, Knowledge and Practices', in R. Barrow and P. White (eds), *Beyond Liberal Education*, London, Routledge.

Hirst, Paul and Peters, Richard S. (1970) *The Logic of Education*, London, Routledge.

Hobbs, Thomas (1968) *Leviathan*, London, Pelican.

Hodgson, Geoffrey (1999) *Economics and Utopia: Why the Learning Society is Not the End of History*, London, Routledge.

Holt, John (1984) *How Children Learn*, London, Pelican.

Hume, David ([1740] 1978) *A Treatise of Human Nature*, edited by P.H. Nidditch, Oxford, Oxford University Press.

Jonathan, Ruth (1997) *Illusory Freedoms*, Oxford, Blackwell.

Kant, I. (1948) *Groundwork of the Metaphysics*, London, Hutchinson.

Kleinig, John (1982) *Philosophical Issues in Education*, London, Croom Helm.

Kymlicka, Will (1995a) *Liberalism, Community and Culture*, Oxford, Clarendon Press.

—— (1995b) *Multicultural Citizenship*, Oxford, Clarendon Press.

Levinson, Meira (2000) *The Demands of Liberal Education*, Oxford, Oxford University Press.

Lum, Gerard (1999) 'Where's the Competence in Competence-based Education and Training?', *Journal of Philosophy of Education*, 33, 3: 403–418.

Lytton, H. (1971) *Creativity in Education*, London, Routledge.

McLaughlin, Terence H. (2000) 'Citizenship Education in England: The Crick Report and Beyond', *Journal of Philosophy of Education*, 34, 4: 541–570.

Marx, Karl ([1887] 1970a) *Capital*, London, Lawrence and Wishart.

Mill, John Stuart ([1859] 1968) *On Liberty* (ed.) A.D. Lindsay, London, Dent.

—— ([1863] 1910) *Utilitarianism*, London, Dent.

Mulhall, Stephen (1998) 'Political Liberalism and Civic Education', *Journal of Philosophy of Education*, 32, 2: 161–176.

Mulhall, Stephen and Swift, Adam (1996) *Liberals and Communitarians: A Revised Edition*, Oxford, Blackwell.

Nagel, Thomas (1991) *Equality and Partiality*, Oxford, Oxford University Press.

National Advisory Committee on Creative and Cultural Education (1999) *All Our Futures: Creativity, Culture and Education*, London, HMSO.

Newton-Smith, William H. (1981) *The Rationality of Science*, London, Routledge.

Norman, Richard (1994) 'I Did it My Way: Some Thoughts on Autonomy', *Journal of Philosophy of Education*, 28, 1: 25–34.

Peters, Richard S. (ed.) (1966) *The Philosophy of Education*, Oxford, Oxford University Press.

Phillips, Melanie (1996) *All Must Have Prizes*, London, Little and Brown.

Prais, Sig (1995) *Productivity, Education and Training: An International Perspective*, Cambridge, Cambridge University Press.

Pring, Richard (1992) 'Standards and Quality in Education', *British Journal of Educational Studies*, 40, 3: 4–22.

—— (1995) *Closing the Gap: Liberal Education and Vocational Preparation*, London, Hodder and Stoughton.

QCA (1998) *Education for Citizenship and the Teaching of Democracy in Schools* (The Crick Report), London, QCA.

Rawls, John (1971) *A Theory of Justice*, Cambridge, MA, Belknap Press.

—— (1985) 'Justice as Fairness: Political not Metaphysical', *Philosophy and Public Affairs*, 14, 3: 223–251.

—— (1993) *Political Liberalism*, Oxford, Oxford University Press.

—— (1999) *A Theory of Justice*, 2nd edn, Oxford, Oxford University Press.

Raz, Joseph (1986) *The Morality of Freedom*, Oxford, The Clarendon Press.

Rousseau, Jean-Jacques ([1762] 1910) *Emile or Education*, translated by Barbara Foxley, London, Dent.

Ryle, Gilbert (1949) *The Concept of Mind*, London, Hutchinson.

—— (1974) 'Intelligence and Logic of the Nature-Nurture Issue: Reply to J.P.White', *Proceedings of the Philosophy of Education Society*, 8, 1: 52–60.

Sandel, Michael (1998) *Liberalism and the Limits of Justice*, Cambridge, Cambridge University Press.

Scarre, Geoffrey (1997) *Utilitarianism*, London, Routledge.

Scheffler, Israel (1973) 'The Concept of Teaching', in I. Scheffler (ed.), *Reason and Teaching*, London, Routledge.

Schopenhauer, Arthur (1883) *The World as Will and Idea*, vols. 1–3, London, Routledge.

Schumpeter, Joseph (1976) *Capitalism, Socialism and Democracy*, London, Routledge.

Scruton, Roger (1998) *An Intelligent Person's Guide to Modern Culture*, London, Duckworth.

Smart, J.J.C. (1973) 'An Outline of a System of Utilitarian Ethics', reprinted in J.J.C.

Smart and B. Williams (eds), *Utilitarianism: For and Against*, Cambridge, Cambridge University Press.

Smith, Adam ([1776] 1981) *The Wealth of Nations*, Indianapolis, Liberty Fund.

Smith, Frank (1985) *Reading*, Cambridge, Cambridge University Press.

Smith, Richard (1987) 'Skills: The Middle Way', *Journal of Philosophy of Education*, 21, 2: 196–202.

Streeck, Wolfgang (1992) *Social Institutions and Economic Performance*, London, Sage.

Sutherland, G. (ed.) (1973) *Arnold and Education*, Harmondsworth, Penguin.

Taylor, Frederick (1911) *The Principles of Scientific Management*, New York, Norton.

Tooley, James (1996) *Education without the State*, London, Institute of Economic Affairs.

—— (1998) 'The "neo-liberal" Critique of State Intervention in Education: Reply to Winch', *Journal of Philosophy of Education*, 32, 2: 107–121.

—— (2000) *Reclaiming Education*, London, Cassell.

Tooley, James and Darby, Doug (1998) *Educational Research: A Critique*, London, Ofsted.

Turner, Martin (1990) *Sponsored Reading Failure: An Object Lesson*, London, Warlington Park School Education Unit.

Varoufakis, Y. and Hargreaves-Heap, S. (1995) *An Introduction to Game Theory*, London, Routledge.

Walton, Kendall (1990) *Mimesis as Make-believe*, Cambridge, MA, Harvard University Press.

Weil, Simone (1958) *Oppression and Liberty*, London, Routledge.

White, John (1968) 'Creativity and Education', *British Journal of Educational Studies*, 16, 2: 123–134.

—— (1973) *Towards a Compulsory Curriculum*, London, Routledge.

—— (1982) *The Aims of Education Restated*, London, Routledge.

—— (1988) 'Two National Curricula – Baker's and Stalin's: Towards a Liberal Alternative', *British Journal of Educational Studies*, 36, 2: 218–231.

—— (1990) *Education and the Good Life*, London, Routledge.

—— (1995) *Education and Well-being in a Secular Universe*, London, Institute of Education.

—— (1997) *Education and the End of Work*, London, Kogan Page.

—— (1999) 'Thinking About Assessment', *Journal of Philosophy of Education*, 34, 2: 201–212.

—— (2003) 'Five Critical Stances Towards Liberal Philosophy of Education in Britain', *Journal of Philosophy of Education*, 37, 1: 147–184.

Williams, Kevin (1998) 'Assessment and the Challenge of Scepticism', in David Carr (ed.), *Education, Knowledge and Truth*, London, Routledge.

—— (2000) *Why Teach Foreign Languages in Schools?*, London, Philosophy of Education Society of Great Britain.

Winch, Christopher (1990) *Language, Ability and Educational Achievement*, New York, Routledge.

—— (1996) *Quality and Education*, Oxford, Blackwell.

—— (1998) *The Philosophy of Human Learning*, London, Routledge.

—— (2000a) *Education, Work and Social Capital*, London, Routledge.

—— (2000b) *New Labour and the Future of Training*, London, Philosophy of Education Society of Great Britain.

—— (2002) 'Strong Autonomy and Education', *Educational Theory*, 52, 1: 27–42.

Winch, Christopher and Clarke, Linda (2003) '"Front-Loaded" Vocational Education

Versus Lifelong Learning. A Critique of Current UK Government Policy', *Oxford Review of Education*, 29, 2: 239–252.

Wiseman, Stephen (ed.) (1973) *Intelligence and Ability*, London, Penguin.

Wolff, J. (1982) 'Aesthetic Judgement and Sociological Analysis', reprinted in S. Sims (ed.) (1992) *Art: Context and Value*, Milton Keynes, Open University Press.

Woodhead, Martin (1985) 'Preschool Education has Long-term Effects, but Can They be Generalised?', *Oxford Review of Education*, 11, 2: 133–156.

Woods, Ronald and Barrow, Robin (1975) *Introduction to the Philosophy of Education*, London, Methuen.

Index